Processing 2: Creative Programming Cookbook

Over 90 highly-effective recipes to unleash your creativity with interactive art, graphics, computer vision, 3D, and more

Jan Vantomme

BIRMINGHAM - MUMBAI

Processing 2: Creative Programming Cookbook

First published: September 2012

Production Reference: 1100912

Published by Packt Publishing Ltd.
Livery Place
35 Livery Street
Birmingham B3 2PB, UK.

ISBN 978-1-849517-94-2

www.packtpub.com

Cover Image by Jan Vantomme (http://www.cloudswimmers.com/)

Credits

Author

Jan Vantomme

Reviewers

Dr. Bryan, Wai-ching CHUNG

Frederik Vanhoutte

Acquisition Editor

Kartikey Pandey

Lead Technical Editor

Kedar Bhat

Technical Editors

Madhuri Das

Kirti Pujari

Copy Editor

Brandt D'Mello

Project Coordinator

Yashodhan Dere

Proofreader

Mario Cecere

Indexer

Hemangini Bari

Production Coordinator

Arvindkumar Gupta

Cover Work

Arvindkumar Gupta

About the Author

Jan Vantomme is a computational designer and artist based in Ghent, Belgium. He runs Cloudswimmers, a small studio with a focus on computational and interaction design. Jan has been using Processing since the early beta versions. He taught the subject at a university college both as faculty staff and as a guest professor. He wrote some Processing libraries to work with colors and shapes in an easy way. Jan also co-founded Processing Ghent, a community for creative coders in Belgium. They organize free lectures and workshops on Processing.

Over the past few years, I've grown a lot as an artist and as a programmer. Without Processing and its amazing community, this book wouldn't have been possible. I'd like to thank the people I've learned from and those who inspired and supported me. Here they are, in no particular order:

Golan Levin, Jan Pillaert, Elise Elsacker, Holger Lippmann, Marcin Ignac, Johan Van Looveren, Ira Greenberg, Andreas Schlegel, Andres Colubri, Stef Bourdon, Ryan Alexander, Matt Pearson, Bert Balcaen, Daniel Shiffman, Andreas Schlegel, Joshua Noble, Casey Reas, Julien Deswaef, Matthew Plummer-Fernandez, Filip Daniels, Jer Thorp, Jessica Rosenkrantz, David Bollinger, Marie-Laure Delaby, Leander Herzog, Corneel Cannaerts, Kim Asendorf, Frederik Vanhoutte, Simon Geilfus, Jared Tarbell, Inge Gobert, Spencer Pieters, Ben Fry, Jonathan McCabe, Andreas Köberle, Marius Watz, Kasper Jordaens, Robert Hodgin, Karsten Schmidt, and John Maeda.

I would also like to thank iMAL and Timelab for organizing workshops on Processing and Arduino, and DOK for letting us use their space for the Processing Ghent meetings.

About the Reviewers

Dr. Bryan, Wai-ching CHUNG is the Assistant Professor of Interactive Art in the Academy of Visual Arts, Hong Kong Baptist University. He is also the founding consultant of the interactive media design company DBIS Interactive (http://www.dbisinteractive.com) in Hong Kong. Dr. Chung obtained his doctoral degree in Fine Arts, master's degree in Multimedia Design, and bachelor's degree in Computer Science. Apart from academic and consultation works, he has produced interactive artworks that have been widely exhibited in Asia and Europe. Currently, he is developing open source software libraries for the Processing community. His works are documented on his personal blog at http://www.magicandlove.com.

Frederik Vanhoutte is a medical radiation physicist with a PhD in experimental solid state physics. When rain hits the windscreen, he sees tracks of alpha particles trace in cells. When he pulls the plug in the bath tub, he stays to watch the little whirlpool. When he sits at the kitchen table, he plays with the glasses to see the caustics. At a candlelight dinner, he stares into the flame. Sometimes at night, he finds himself in front of the computer. When he finally blinks, a mess of code is drawing random structures on the screen. He spends the rest of the night staring.

Working with Processing since 2004, creative coding fuels his curiosity of physical, biological, and computational systems. He shares his constructs on his website wblut.com. Recently, his hemesh Processing library has been gaining a small following for the creation and manipulation of 3D meshes.

www.PacktPub.com

Support files, eBooks, discount offers and more

You might want to visit www.PacktPub.com for support files and downloads related to your book.

Did you know that Packt offers eBook versions of every book published, with PDF and ePub files available? You can upgrade to the eBook version at www.PacktPub.com and as a print book customer, you are entitled to a discount on the eBook copy. Get in touch with us at service@packtpub.com for more details.

At www.PacktPub.com, you can also read a collection of free technical articles, sign up for a range of free newsletters and receive exclusive discounts and offers on Packt books and eBooks.

http://PacktLib.PacktPub.com

Do you need instant solutions to your IT questions? PacktLib is Packt's online digital book library. Here, you can access, read and search across Packt's entire library of books.

Why Subscribe?

- ▸ Fully searchable across every book published by Packt
- ▸ Copy and paste, print and bookmark content
- ▸ On demand and accessible via web browser

Free Access for Packt account holders

If you have an account with Packt at www.PacktPub.com, you can use this to access PacktLib today and view nine entirely free books. Simply use your login credentials for immediate access.

Table of Contents

Preface

Processing is probably the best-known creative coding environment that helps you bridge the gap between programming and art. It enables designers, artists, architects, students, and many others, to explore graphics programming and computational art in an easy way, thus helping boost creativity.

Processing 2: Creative Programming Cookbook will guide you to explore and experience the open source Processing language and environment, helping you discover advanced features and exciting possibilities with this programming environment, like never before. You'll learn the basics of 2D and 3D graphics programming, and then quickly move up to advanced topics, such as audio and video visualization, computer vision, and much more, with this comprehensive guide.

Since its birth in 2001, Processing has grown a lot. What started out as a project by Ben Fry and Casey Reas has now become a widely used graphics programming language.

Processing 2 has a lot of new and exciting features. This cookbook will guide you through exploring the completely new and cool graphics engine and video library. Using the recipes in this cookbook, you will be able to build interactive art for desktop computers, the Internet, and even Android devices! You don't even have to use a keyboard or mouse to interact with the art you make. The book's next-gen technologies will teach you how to design interactions with a webcam or a microphone! Isn't that amazing?

Processing 2: Creative Programming Cookbook will guide you to explore the Processing language and environment using practical and useful recipes.

What this book covers

Chapter 1, Getting Started with Processing 2, takes a look at installing Processing on your computer and creating your first interactive sketch.

Chapter 2, Drawing Text, Curves, and Shapes in 2D, covers the basics of 2D drawing. We'll take a look at how we can use colors, typography, and images.

Chapter 3, Drawing in 3D—Lights, Camera, and Action!, explores the third dimension. You'll learn how to draw basic 3D shapes and how you can use lights to add some extra depth to your 3D scene.

Chapter 4, Working with Data, will teach you how to load data from text files and parse it to make it useful in your sketch. We also explore some datatypes that will be useful for storing data.

Chapter 5, Exporting from Processing, covers everything to get your work out in the world. You'll learn to save your sketches as an image, PDF file, or standalone application.

Chapter 6, Working with Video, explores how you can work with video and how you can manipulate it to create something interesting.

Chapter 7, Audio Visualization, will show you how to use the Minim library. We'll take a look at how we can visualize audio, and create some basic instruments.

Chapter 8, Exploring Computer Vision, will teach you how computer vision works with Processing. We'll take a look at blob tracking and color tracking and will explore the basics of OpenCV.

Chapter 9, Exploring JavaScript Mode, will show you how you can use your freshly acquired Processing skills to create interactive sketches for the web.

Chapter 10, Exploring Android Mode, covers how you can use Processing to create interactive applications for Android smartphones and tablets.

Chapter 11, Using Processing with Other Editors, shows you how you can use Processing with Eclipse and IntelliJ IDEA. We also take a look at how you can create your own libraries and tools to use with Processing.

What you need for this book

The software you need for the biggest part of the book is Processing, and can be downloaded at http://processing.org/.

For some chapters, you'll need to download some extra software. For *Chapter 10*, you need the Android SDK, which can be downloaded at `http://developer.android.com/sdk/index.html`. For *Chapter 11*, you'll need some other editors to work with Processing. Eclipse can be downloaded at `http://eclipse.org/` and IntelliJ IDEA at `http://www.jetbrains.com/idea/`.

If you need to download or install extra libraries, fonts, or other files, the recipe will mention where you can find what you need.

Who this book is for

This book targets creative professionals, visual artists, designers, and students who have basic knowledge of the Processing development environment and who want to discover the next level of Processing—anyone with a creative practice who wants to use computation in their design process. A basic understanding of programming is assumed. However, this book is also recommended to the non-artistic looking to expand their graphics and artistic skills.

Conventions

In this book, you will find a number of styles of text that distinguish between different kinds of information. Here are some examples of these styles and an explanation of their meaning.

Code words in text are shown as follows: "The `size()` function sets the dimensions of your sketch window."

A block of code is set as follows:

```
void setup()
{
  size( 640, 480 );
  smooth();
}

void draw()
{
  background(255);
```

New terms and **important words** are shown in bold. Words that you see on the screen, in menus or dialog boxes for example, appear in the text like this: "Click on the **Run** button to start Processing."

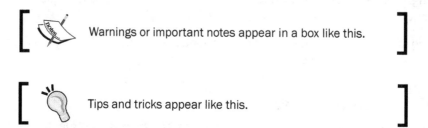

Warnings or important notes appear in a box like this.

Tips and tricks appear like this.

Reader feedback

Feedback from our readers is always welcome. Let us know what you think about this book—what you liked or may have disliked. Reader feedback is important for us to develop titles that you really get the most out of.

To send us general feedback, simply send an e-mail to feedback@packtpub.com, and mention the book title via the subject of your message.

If there is a topic that you have expertise in and you are interested in either writing or contributing to a book, see our author guide on www.packtpub.com/authors.

Customer support

Now that you are the proud owner of a Packt book, we have a number of things to help you to get the most from your purchase.

Downloading the example code

You can download the example code files for all Packt books you have purchased from your account at http://www.PacktPub.com. If you purchased this book elsewhere, you can visit http://www.PacktPub.com/support and register to have the files e-mailed directly to you.

Errata

Although we have taken every care to ensure the accuracy of our content, mistakes do happen. If you find a mistake in one of our books—maybe a mistake in the text or the code—we would be grateful if you would report this to us. By doing so, you can save other readers from frustration and help us improve subsequent versions of this book. If you find any errata, please report them by visiting http://www.packtpub.com/support, selecting your book, clicking on the **errata submission form** link, and entering the details of your errata. Once your errata are verified, your submission will be accepted and the errata will be uploaded on our website, or added to any list of existing errata, under the Errata section of that title. Any existing errata can be viewed by selecting your title from http://www.packtpub.com/support.

Piracy

Piracy of copyright material on the Internet is an ongoing problem across all media. At Packt, we take the protection of our copyright and licenses very seriously. If you come across any illegal copies of our works, in any form, on the Internet, please provide us with the location address or website name immediately so that we can pursue a remedy.

Please contact us at copyright@packtpub.com with a link to the suspected pirated material.

We appreciate your help in protecting our authors, and our ability to bring you valuable content.

Questions

You can contact us at questions@packtpub.com if you are having a problem with any aspect of the book, and we will do our best to address it.

1
Getting Started with Processing 2

In this chapter we will cover:

- ▶ Installing Processing on your computer
- ▶ Exploring the Processing Development Environment
- ▶ Installing libraries
- ▶ Installing tools
- ▶ Switching modes
- ▶ Understanding the coordinate system
- ▶ Writing your first Processing sketch
- ▶ Using math functions
- ▶ Responding to mouse events
- ▶ Responding to keyboard events

Introduction

In this chapter, we'll take a look at the very basics of Processing. You'll learn how to install Processing on your computer, and extend it with libraries and tools. We'll also take a glimpse at the different modes that are available in Processing 2. These things aren't very exciting, but you need to know about them before you can start creating interactive art.

But don't worry, you'll have written your first Processing sketches by the time you reach the end of the chapter. You will learn more about the structure of a Processing sketch, and we'll use some math along the way. These sketches will also teach you the basics of interaction between humans and computers. We'll use the mouse and keyboard to create simple, yet somewhat useful applications. You'll notice that programming in the Processing language probably isn't as hard as you may have thought.

Installing Processing on your computer

Processing is an open source programming language and environment. It can be used to create images, interactive installations, smartphone applications, and even 3D printed objects. Just about anything you can imagine. In this recipe, we'll take a look at installing Processing on Mac OS X, Windows, and Linux.

Getting ready

Download Processing 2 for your operating system at `http://processing.org/download/`. Processing is available for Windows, Mac OS X, and Linux. Processing for Windows comes in two flavors, one with Java and one without. Download the one with Java if you aren't sure which one to choose.

How to do it...

- **Windows**: Unzip the file you've downloaded to `C:\Program Files`. You'll find the Processing application at `C:\Program Files\Processing\`. You might want to create a desktop shortcut to this app so it's easily available.

- **Mac OS X**: Unzip the file you've downloaded and drag the Processing application to your `Applications` folder.

- **Linux**: Unzip the folder to your `Documents` folder. Processing for Linux is a shell script. You can double-click this script and click the **Run** button to start Processing.

How it works...

The Processing language is built on top of Java, so you'll need a Java runtime on your computer for it to work. All versions of Mac OS X prior to 10.7 had a Java runtime installed by default. Starting with 10.7, Apple removed this. But don't worry. When you start Processing for the first time, the OS will ask you to install a Java runtime if you haven't done that already.

Processing for Windows and Linux comes with a java directory that contains everything you need to run Processing. You can however choose to use another Java runtime if you've installed one on your machine. But you should only do this if you are an advanced user and familiar with Java on one of these platforms.

There's more...

Processing uses a folder called the Sketchbook, where you will keep your sketches, libraries, and tools. Best practice is to keep this Sketchbook folder in the standard place for your OS.

- **Mac OS X**: /username/Documents/Processing/
- **Windows**: C:\Documents and Settings\username\My Documents\ Processing\
- **Linux**: /home/username/sketchbook/

Exploring the Processing Development Environment

When you start to work with a new application, it's important to understand the interface. In this recipe, we'll take a look at the **Processing Development Environment**, sometimes referred to as **PDE**.

How to do it...

This is the easiest thing you'll do in this book. Just open the Processing application. The following screenshot shows you what the PDE looks like on Mac OS X:

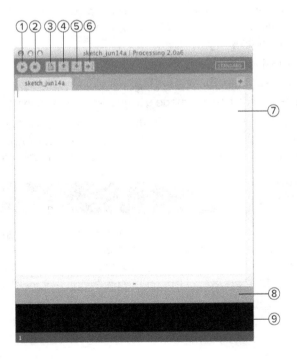

How it works...

When you open the Processing app, you'll notice that the PDE is a very basic programming environment. If you are an experienced programmer, you might miss a lot of features. The PDE was designed like this, so that people without any programming experience can get started with exploring code without having to worry about project settings, or learning a difficult interface. Let's take a look at the different interface elements.

1. This is the run button. If you click this button, it will compile your code, and run your sketch in a new window. The shortcut for running your code is *Cmd + R* on the Mac, and *Ctrl + R* on Windows and Linux. Alternatively, you can hold down the *Shift* key while clicking this button to present your sketch. This will run your sketch centered on a gray fullscreen background.

2. The stop button will terminate your sketch. You can also press the *Esc* key on your keyboard.

3. Clicking the new button will create a new Processing sketch in the current window. If you want to create a sketch in a new window, you can use the **File | New** menu.

4. The open button will open a menu with the names of all sketches in your sketchbook folder. This will open a sketch in the current window. If you want to open a sketch in a new window, you can use the **File | Open** menu.

5. The save button will open a dialog to save your sketch.

6. The export button will compile your sketch as an application. Holding down the *Shift* key will export your sketch as a Java Applet. You'll learn more about exporting your sketches in the *Exporting applications* in *Chapter 5, Exporting from Processing* recipe.

7. This is the text editor where you will type your code.

8. The message area is used by Processing to display messages when you save or export our sketch, or when you made a syntax error while coding.

9. The console is used to display more detailed error messages. The output of the `print()` and `println()` functions will also appear here. You'll learn more about these functions in the *Using math functions* recipe later in this chapter.

Installing libraries

The core functionality of Processing is very basic. This was done by design, to make it easy for everyone to get started using it. If you need to do something that's not available in Processing, you can use a **library** that adds the functionality you need. One of the new features in Processing 2 is the **Library Manager**. This allows you to install new libraries in the easy way.

Getting ready

There is an overview of the available Processing libraries on the Processing website at
`http://processing.org/reference/libraries/`. You'll find the documentation of the
libraries included with Processing and a list with contributed libraries. There are libraries to
work with 3D, computer vision, geometry, and a lot more.

How to do it...

You can open the library manager by using this menu: **Sketch | Import Library... | Add
Library...**. This will give you a list of available libraries. To install the library you need to select
it from the list and click on the **Install** button. Processing will install the library in the libraries
folder of your sketchbook.

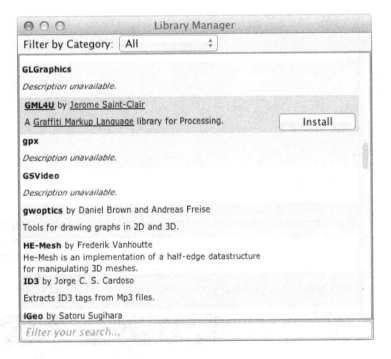

Unfortunately, not all libraries are included in this list. Some of the older libraries will probably
still work in Processing 2, but the developer might not have added the new functionality to
install the library through the **Library Manager**. In that case, you'll need to install the library
manually. Don't worry; this is not as hard as it sounds.

You should download the library from the website of the developer and unzip it. Drag this folder to the `libraries` folder inside your sketchbook. Libraries are structured in a (predefined) way. If the library is not structured like this, it won't work. The main library folder usually contains four subfolders: `examples`, `library`, `reference`, and `src`. The `examples` folder contains Processing sketches the developer made to show how the library works. The `library` folder contains the compiled library code that will be imported into your sketch. The `reference` folder stores the documentation on how to use the library. The `src` folder contains the source code of the library. This might be handy for advanced users to learn how the library works and modify it as per their needs.

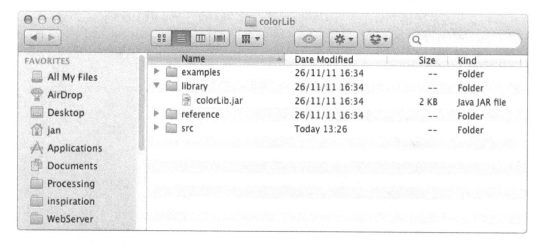

How it works...

The folder structure for libraries is important for Processing to find the library. The main folder for the colorLib library is named **colorLib**. Inside the **library** folder within that directory, you'll find a file named **colorLib.jar**. This JAR file will be included in your applet or application when you export your sketch. You can add import libraries into your sketch by going to the **Sketch | Import Library...** menu and select the library you want.

Installing tools

Processing **tools** are little applications that extend the PDE. Processing comes with a standard set of tools: a color selector, a tool to create fonts, a tool to create movies, and some other useful things.

Getting ready

There is an overview of available tools on the Processing website at `http://processing.org/reference/tools/`. This overview includes all standard tools and tools made by people from the Processing community. At the moment, there aren't that many tools available, but the number of quality tools might grow in the future.

How to do it...

Processing 2 has a new feature to install tools in an easy way: the **Tool Manager**. You can find the **Tool Manager** by going to **Tools | Add Tool...**. The Tool Manager works the same way as the Library Manager we've discussed in the *Installing libraries* recipe. Just like with libraries, not all tools are available in the **Tool Manager**. If you find a tool online, you can install it manually in the `tools` directory. This procedure is the same as installing a library manually. The **Tool Manager** looks as shown in the following screenshot:

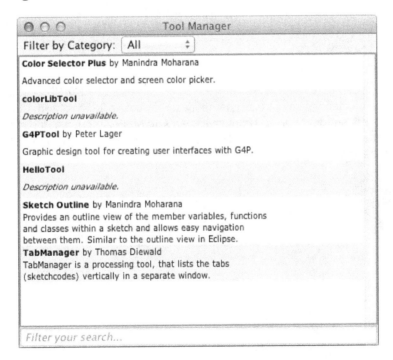

How it works...

Tools are installed in the `tools` directory in your sketchbook. Each tool directory usually contains two directories, one for the tool, which contains the tool JAR file, and one with the Java source code. This JAR file is executed from the tool menu.

Switching modes

When Processing first came out, there was only the standard Java mode. But a lot has changed over recent years. The Processing language was ported to JavaScript by John Resig to show the capabilities of the HTML5 canvas element. Processing 2 also enables you to create apps for the Android operating system.

Getting ready

Open the Processing app. You probably already did that, since you're reading this book.

How to do it...

In the upper-right corner of the PDE, you'll see a button with the text **STANDARD**. If you click it, you'll get a small menu to select the other modes. Processing 2 comes with three modes: **Standard**, **Android**, and **JavaScript**. There is also an **Add Mode...** option in the menu, which will open the **Mode Manager**. This Mode Manager works in a similar way to the Library Manager and the Tool Manager.

How it works...

If you run a sketch in **Standard** mode, the PDE will compile your code and run it as a Java applet. This mode is useful if you want to create native applications that will run on a computer. Running a sketch in **JavaScript** mode will start a local web server on your computer, and open your default browser so you can see the sketch run within a HTML5 page. **Android** mode will run the sketch in the Android Emulator or on your Android device.

 You'll need to install the Android SDK to make this work. The color scheme of the PDE is also different in Android mode, so it's a little easier to see in which mode you are.

See also

This book also covers the new JavaScript and Android modes in depth. You can learn all about it in *Chapter 9, JavaScript Mode*, and *Chapter 10, Exploring Android Mode*.

Understanding the coordinate system

Before you can draw things to the screen, you need to know how the coordinate system works. Design applications might use a different point for the origin of their drawing surface. For instance, Photoshop uses the upper-left corner as (0,0), while Illustrator uses the bottom-left corner as (0,0).

Getting ready

Open Processing and create a new sketch.

How to do it...

Type this line of code in the Processing editor and press the run button. You can also use *Ctrl + R* (Windows, Linux) or *Cmd + R* (Mac OS X) to run your sketch.

```
size( 400, 300 );
```

How it works...

Processing uses the upper-left corner for the origin of the window. The `size()` function sets the dimensions of your sketch window. The first parameter is used to set the value of the system variable `width`, the second parameter is used to set the value of the system variable `height`.

Imagine that you want to draw a point at the bottom-right corner of the window. If you were to draw that point at (400, 300), you won't see anything on your screen. You need to draw your point at (*width-1, height-1*) to make it visible on screen. This may look a little strange, but it's actually very logical. If you want to draw a point at the origin, you'll use: `point(0, 0);`. This line of code will fill the first pixel on the first row. As we start counting at 0, the last pixel on that row would be 399, or width-1. The same is true for the height. The following screenshot shows our window of 400 by 300 pixels, divided into squares of 50 x 50 pixels.

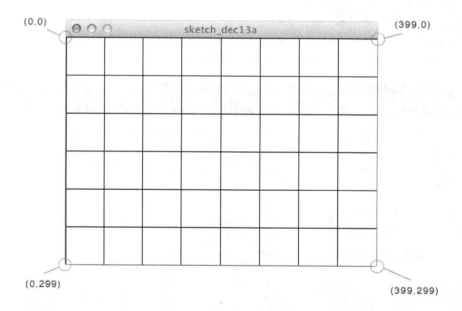

Writing your first Processing sketch

In the previous recipes, you've learned all the boring stuff such as installing Processing and libraries. It's time to get your hands dirty now and write some code.

Getting ready

Create a new Processing sketch and save it as `my_first_sketch` to your sketch folder.

How to do it...

This is the full code for your first sketch. This sketch will draw some lines and points with varying stroke weights.

```
void setup()
{
  size( 640, 480 );
  smooth();
}

void draw()
{
  background(255);

  strokeWeight( 1 );
  point( 20, height/1.5 );
  line( 70, 20, 70, height - 20 );
  strokeWeight( 2 );
  point( 120, height/1.75 );
  line( 170, 20, 170, height - 20 );
  strokeWeight( 4 );
  point( 220, height/2 );
  line( 270, 20, 270, height - 20 );
  strokeWeight( 8 );
  point( 320, height/3 );
  line( 370, 20, 370, height - 20 );
  strokeWeight( 16 );
  point( 420, height/4 );
  line( 470, 20, 470, height - 20 );
  strokeWeight( 32 );
  point( 520, height/5 );
  line( 570, 20, 570, height - 20 );
}
```

If you run the sketch, you'll see the results of your hard work. It will look as shown in the following screenshot:

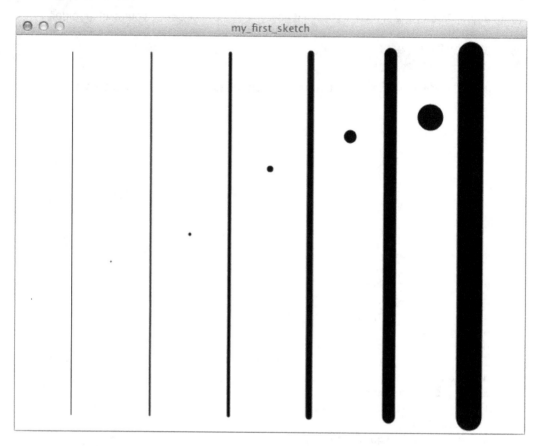

How it works...

In this recipe, you've learned the most basic functions to create a simple Processing sketch. Let's take a deeper look at what these functions do:

- The setup() function is called only once when you run your sketch. You'll use this function to set the size of your sketch, add values to some variables, load images, and so on.

- The draw() function is called continuously, at a rate of 60 frames per second.

- The size() function sets the size of your sketch window. You can use size(screenWidth, screenHeight) to create a sketch with dimensions that match the resolution of your computer screen.

- The `smooth()` function is used to enable anti-aliasing. This means that all your shapes will have a soft edge. If you don't use this function, the shapes will have a more jagged edge.

- The `point()` function is used to draw a point on the screen. The first parameter is the x-coordinate, the second one is the y-coordinate of the point you want to draw.

- The `line()` function is used to draw a line on the screen. To draw a line, you basically need two points to define that line, as you might remember from math class in high school. The first two parameters of this function are the x and y coordinates of the first point, the third and fourth parameters are the x and y coordinates of the second point.

- The `strokeWeight()` function will change the appearance of the shape you'll draw to the screen. The parameter will set the width of the stroke. For example, you can use `strokeWeight(4)` to draw a line with a thickness of 4 pixels.

There's more...

Processing sketches have a specific folder structure. If you save your sketch as `my_first_sketch`, you'll find a folder with this name in your Processing sketchbook. Inside this folder, you'll find a file named `my_first_sketch.pde`. Processing uses this folder structure to keep everything it needs to run the sketch together. This will be very handy when you write more complicated sketches that use more code files, or other data such as images or fonts.

Using math functions

You'll likely use some basic math when writing sketches with Processing. Don't worry if you forgot some of the math you learned in school, the Processing language comes with some handy functions that can do the hard work for you. But you might need to sharpen your math skills if you want to use these functions for some more advanced things such as data visualization.

Getting ready

We're going to write a small sketch that uses some of the math functions. The output of the app will be logged to the console. Start by creating a new sketch and save it as `math_functions.pde`.

How to do it...

This is the full code for the application we are going to write. We'll start by declaring some integer and float variables. The numbers variable is an array of floats containing the values of the variables we declared before. This sketch uses the println() function to log the output of the abs(), ceil(), floor(), round(), sq(), sqrt(), min(), max(), and dist() functions to the console.

```
int x = 177;
int y = -189;
float a = 32.75;
float b = -70.38;

float[] numbers = {a, b, x, y};

println("The absolute value of " + a + " is " + abs(a) );
println("The absolute value of " + b + " is " + abs(b) );
println("The absolute value of " + y + " is " + abs(y) );
println("The closest int value greater than (or equal to) " + x + " is " + ceil(x) );
println("The closest int value greater than (or equal to) " + a + " is " + ceil(a) );
println("The closest int value greater than (or equal to) " + b + " is " + ceil(b) );
println("The closest int value less than (or equal to) " + y + " is " + floor(y) );
println("The closest int value less than (or equal to) " + a + " is " + floor(a) );
println("The closest int value less than (or equal to) " + b + " is " + floor(b) );
println("The closest int value to " + a + " is " + round(a) );
println("The closest int value to " + b + " is " + round(b) );
println("The square number of " + x + " is " + sq(x) );
println("The square number of " + b + " is " + sq(b) );
println("The square root of " + x + " is " + sqrt(x) );
println("The square root of " + a + " is " + sqrt(a) );
println("The square root of " + b + " is " + sqrt(b) );
println("The smallest number in the list {" + a + "," + b + "," + x + "," + y + "} is " + min( numbers ) );
println("The largest number in the list {" + a + "," + b + "," + x + "," + y + "} is " + max( numbers ) );
println("The distance between (" + x + ", " + y + ") and (" + a + ", " + b + ") is " + dist(x, y, a, b ) );
```

If you run the sketch, you'll see that Processing will show an empty gray window of 100 x 100 pixels. This is the standard window size Processing uses if you don't use the `size()` function in a sketch. The output of the application will look as shown in the following screenshot:

```
println("The square number of " + x + " is " + sq(x) );
println("The square number of " + b + " is " + sq(b) );
println("The square root of " + x + " is " + sqrt(x) );
println("The square root of " + a + " is " + sqrt(a) );
println("The square root of " + b + " is " + sqrt(b) );
```

```
Done Saving.
The absolute value of 32.45 is 32.45
The absolute value of -70.38 is 70.38
The absolute value of -189 is 189
The closest int value greater than (or equal to) 177 is 177
The closest int value greater than (or equal to) 32.45 is 33
The closest int value greater than (or equal to) -70.38 is -70
The closest int value less than (or equal to) -189 is -189
The closest int value less than (or equal to) 32.45 is 32
The closest int value less than (or equal to) -70.38 is -71
The closest int value to 32.45 is 32
26
```

How it works...

You've learned a lot of new functions to work with numbers in this recipe. Let's take a look at what they do:

- `abs()` calculates the absolute value of the parameter. The result is always a positive number, so `abs(-189)` will return the number **189**.
- `ceil()` returns the closest integer value, greater than or equal to the value of the parameter. For instance, `ceil(177)` will return **177**, `ceil(-70.38)` will return **-70**.
- `floor()` returns the closest integer value, less than or equal to the value of the parameter. `floor(32.75)` will return **32**, `floor(-70.38)` will return **-71**.
- `round()` returns the closest integer value to the parameter. `round(32.75)` will return the number **33**, `round(-70.38)` will return **-70**.
- `min()` returns the smallest number from the list used as the parameter.
- `max()` returns the largest number from the list used as the parameter.
- `sq()` returns the square of a number. This is the same as multiplying the value of the parameter by itself. Using this function will always result in a positive number.
- `sqrt()` returns the square root of a number. The value of the parameter should always be a positive number. `sqrt(-70.38)` will return **NaN** (short for **Not a Number**).
- `dist()` calculates the distance between two points. The first two parameters are the x and y coordinates of the first point, and the third and fourth parameters are the x and y coordinates of the second point. The `dist()` function uses the distance formula, which is derived from the Pythagorean theorem.

There's more...

The `println()` function is really handy to debug your sketches. You'll use it a lot to log the value of a variable to the console. For instance, `println(a)` will log the value of variable a to the console. But you can also combine variables and even other functions inside the `println()` function, just like we did in the code for this small sketch. Let's take a look at how you can do this.

```
println( x + y );
```

This line will print the number **-12** to the console. The + operator has precedence over the `println()` function, so the calculation will be performed first, before the `println()` function is executed.

```
println( x + " " + y );
```

This line will print **177 -189** to the console, and is the easiest way to print the values of the two variables to the console. In this example, the + sign inside the `println()` function is used to combine the values of the two variables together with the space between the two quotes into a variable of the type `String`.

Responding to mouse events

When you interact with a computer, you'll probably use a mouse. This is a standard input device on all computers that use a **graphical user interface** (**GUI**). The mouse became popular in the 1980s when Apple released the Macintosh. Most people know how to use a mouse, or trackpad, so you can easily use this to create art for people to interact with.

How to do it...

This is the full code for the sketch.

 Here, the `draw()` function is empty, as we'll do all the drawing with the mouse functions. We do need to add the draw function though, as it is used to make our app run continuously. If we leave it out of the code, the code in `setup()` will only run once and the app won't be interactive.

```
void setup()
{
  size( 640, 480 );
  smooth();
  background( 255 );
}
```

```
void draw()
{
  // empty, but we need it to create an app that runs in the
continuous mode.
}

void mousePressed()
{
  if ( mouseButton == RIGHT ) {
    background( 255 );
  }
}

void mouseMoved()
{
  stroke( 0, 64 );
  strokeWeight( 1 );
  fill( 255, 32 );
  float d = dist( mouseX, mouseY, pmouseX, pmouseY );
  constrain( d, 8, 100 );
  ellipse( mouseX, mouseY, d, d );
}

void mouseDragged()
{
  stroke( 0 );
  float d = dist( mouseX, mouseY, pmouseX, pmouseY );
  constrain( d, 0, 100 );
  float w = map( d, 0, 100, 1, 10 );
  strokeWeight( w );
  line( mouseX, mouseY, pmouseX, pmouseY );
}

void mouseReleased()
{
  noStroke();
  fill( 255, 16 );
  rect( 0, 0, width, height );
}

void mouseClicked()
{
  fill( 255, 0, 0, 128 );
  float d = random( 20, 200 );
  ellipse( mouseX, mouseY, d, d );
}
```

After typing this code, you can run your sketch by clicking the run button or using the shortcut *Cmd + R* on the Mac or *Ctrl + R* on Windows and Linux. You can now start drawing with your mouse. When you move your mouse, you'll leave a trail of circles. When you press the mouse button and release it, you'll draw a red circle. When you move the mouse while pressing the left mouse button, you'll draw a black stroke. You can use the right mouse button to erase the screen and start all over again. The output of the application might look similar to the following screenshot:

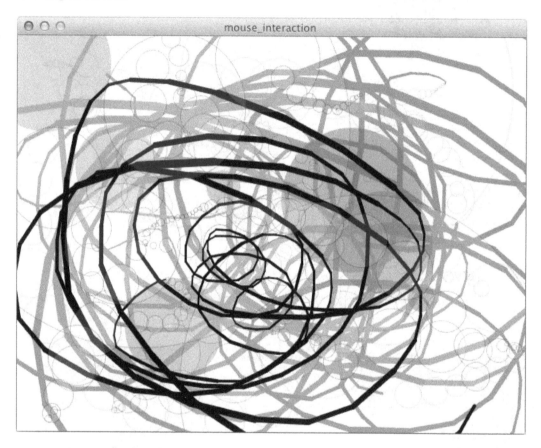

How it works...

There are five functions and six system variables you can use to track mouse interaction in your sketch:

> ► The `mouseClicked()` function is executed when you click a mouse button. This means pressing the button and releasing it. In the application you just made, this function was used to draw the transparent red circle.

- The `mouseDragged()` function is executed when you press a mouse button and move the mouse while the button is pressed. This function is used to draw the lines in our sketch.

- The `mouseMoved()` function is called every time the mouse is moved while no buttons are pressed. In our sketch, this leaves a trail of white transparent circles with a transparent black border.

- The `mousePressed()` function is called when you press the button on your mouse. We use this function, together with the system variable mouseButton, to clear the screen if the right mouse button was pressed.

- The `mouseReleased()` function is called when you release the mouse button. We used this function in our sketch to draw a transparent white rectangle with the size of the window on top of everything.

- The system variable `mouseX` contains the current x coordinate of the mouse within the sketch window. This variable is updated every frame.

- The system variable `mouseY` contains the current y coordinate of the mouse within the sketch window. This variable is updated every frame.

- The system variable `pmouseX` contains the x coordinate of the mouse in the previous frame. This variable is updated every frame.

- The system variable `pmouseY` contains the y coordinate of the mouse in the previous frame. This variable is updated every frame.

- The system variable `mousePressed` is a boolean variable that keeps track if a mouse button is pressed or not. The value of this variable is true if a mouse button is pressed and false if no buttons are pressed.

- The system variable `mouseButton` is a variable used to keep track of which mouse button is pressed. The value of this variable can be `LEFT`, `RIGHT`, or `CENTER`.

Responding to keyboard events

Another form of human-computer interaction is the keyboard. Next to the mouse, this is also one of the best-known devices to interact with computers. You can easily detect when a user presses a key, or releases it again, with Processing. One of the great things is that you can assign keys programmatically to execute pieces of code for you. This is one of the easiest ways to create a simple user-interface with Processing. For instance, you could use the *D* key to toggle a debug mode in your app, or the *S* key to save the drawing you made as an image.

How to do it...

We'll start by declaring some variables and writing the `setup()` and `draw()` functions. In this recipe, we'll write a basic Processing sketch that will change the values of the variables we've declared when we press certain keys on the keyboard.

```
int x;
int y;
int r;
color c;
boolean drawStroke;

void setup()
{
  size( 480, 320 );
  smooth();
  strokeWeight( 2 );

  x = width/2;
  y = height/2;
  r = 80;
  c = color( 255, 0, 0 );
  drawStroke = true;
}

void draw()
{
  background( 255 );

  if ( drawStroke == true ) {
    stroke( 0 );
  } else {
    noStroke();
  }

  fill( c );
  ellipse( x, y, r*2, r*2 );
}
```

The next code we'll write are the functions that will take care of the keyboard events. There are three functions we can use: `keyPressed()`, `keyReleased()`, and `keyTyped()`.

```
void keyPressed()
{
  if ( key == CODED ) {
```

```
    if ( keyCode == RIGHT ) {
      x += 10;
    } else if ( keyCode == LEFT ) {
      x -= 10;
    } else if ( keyCode == UP ) {
      y -= 10;
    } else if ( keyCode == DOWN ) {
      y += 10;
    }
  }

  x = constrain( x, r, width-r );
  y = constrain( y, r, height-r );

}

void keyReleased()
{
  switch ( key ) {
    case 'r':
      c = color( 255, 0, 0 );
      break;
    case 'g':
      c = color( 0, 255, 0 );
      break;
    case 'b':
      c = color( 0, 0, 255 );
      break;
    case 'c':
      c = color( 0, 255, 255 );
      break;
    case 'm':
      c = color( 255, 0, 255 );
      break;
    case 'y':
      c = color( 255, 255, 0 );
      break;
    default:
      break;
  }
}
void keyTyped()
{
  if ( key == 's' ) {
    drawStroke = !drawStroke;
  }
}
```

The result of this application looks as shown in the following screenshot:

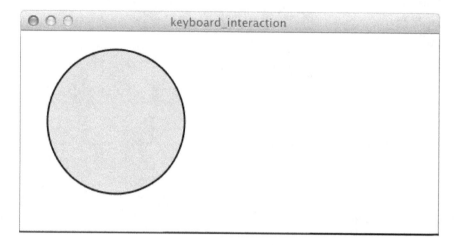

You can use the **arrow keys** to move the ball around. The *S* key will toggle the stroke. The *R, G, B, C, M,* and *Y* keys will change the color of the ball.

How it works...

There are three different functions that catch key events in Processing: `keyPressed()`, `keyReleased()`, and `keyTyped()`. These functions behave a little differently. The `keyPressed()` function is executed when you press a key. You should use this one when you need direct interaction with your application. The `keyReleased()` function is executed when you release the key. This will be useful when you hold a key and change something in your running application when the key is released. The `keyTyped()` function behaves just like the `keyPressed()` function, but ignores all special keys such as the arrow keys, *Enter, Ctrl,* and *Alt*.

▶ The system variable `key` contains the value of the last key that was pressed on the keyboard.

▶ The system variable `keyCode` is used to detect when special keys such as *Shift, Ctrl,* or the arrow keys are pressed. You'll most likely use this one within an if-statement that checks if the key is `CODED`, just like you did in the `keyPressed()` function in the example. The value of `keyCode` can be UP, DOWN, LEFT, RIGHT, ALT, CONTROL, SHIFT, BACKSPACE, TAB, ENTER, RETURN, ESC, or DELETE.

▶ The system variable `keyPressed` is a boolean variable. The value of this variable is true if a key on the keyboard is pressed and false if no keys are pressed. This is a handy variable to use inside the `draw()` function.

▶ The `keyPressed()` function is executed once when you press a key.

▶ The `keyReleased()` function is executed once when you release a key.

▶ The `keyTyped()` function is executed when you type a key. Keys like *Alt*, *Ctrl*, or *Shift* are ignored by this function.

There's more...

You've just learned how to react to single key presses. If you want to do something when a user presses multiple keys (shortcuts such as *Ctrl* + *S* to save an image), it won't work with these standard functions. There is an excellent article on the Processing Wiki that describes strategies for detecting multiple key presses at `http://wiki.processing.org/w/Multiple_key_presses`.

2
Drawing Text, Curves, and Shapes in 2D

In this chapter we will cover:

- ▶ Drawing basic shapes
- ▶ Working with colors
- ▶ Working with images
- ▶ Drawing text
- ▶ Drawing curves
- ▶ Calculating points on a curve
- ▶ Drawing custom shapes
- ▶ Manipulating SVG files
- ▶ Offscreen drawing

Introduction

Now that you've installed Processing on your computer, and written your first sketches, we'll take a look at how you can draw stuff to the screen. We will start with rectangles and circles, and move on to more complex shapes. You'll also learn about working with colors, images, and text.

Drawing basic shapes

In *Chapter 1, Getting Started with Processing 2*, you learned how to draw lines and points in the *Writing my first Processing sketch* recipe. In this recipe, we'll take a look at how you can draw the most basic geometric shapes: rectangles, ellipses, triangles, and quads.

How to do it...

The following is the code for drawing the most basic shapes. The first thing you need to do is to write the `setup()` function and set the window size to 640 by 480 pixels:

```
void setup()
{
  size( 640, 480 );
  smooth();
}
```

The next piece of code is a function that will draw a grid with squares of 10 by 10 pixels. This function will be called in the `draw()` function:

```
void drawGrid()
{
  stroke( 225 );
  for ( int i = 0; i < 64; i++ ) {
    line( i*10, 0, i*10, height );
  }

  for ( int i = 0; i < 48; i++ ) {
    line( 0, i*10, width, i*10 );
  }
}
```

The last thing you need to do is write the `draw()` function. We'll start by setting the background to white, then draw the grid, and finally draw some rectangles, ellipses, triangles, and quads.

```
void draw()
{
  background( 255 );

  drawGrid();

  stroke( 0 );

  // rectangles (yellow)
  fill( 255, 255, 0 );
  rect( 20, 20, 120, 120 );
  rect( 180, 20, 120, 120, 20 );
  rect( 340, 20, 120, 120, 20, 10, 40, 80 );
  rect( 500, 40, 120, 80 );

  // ellipses (red)
```

```
    fill( 255, 0, 0 );
    ellipse( 80, 240, 120, 120 );
    ellipse( 240, 240, 120, 80 );
    ellipse( 400, 240, 80, 120 );

    // triangles (blue)
    fill( 0, 0, 255 );
    triangle( 560, 180, 620, 300, 500, 300 );
    triangle( 40, 340, 140, 460, 20, 420 );

    // quads (cyan)
    fill( 0, 255, 255 );
    quad( 180, 340, 300, 340, 300, 380, 180, 460 );
    quad( 400, 340, 440, 400, 400, 460, 360, 400 );
    quad( 500, 340, 620, 400, 500, 460, 560, 400 );
}
```

If you run the code, the result will look as shown in the following screenshot.

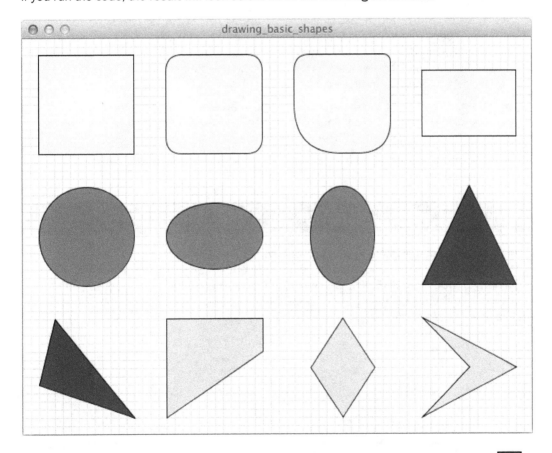

How it works...

The `drawGrid()` function is a custom function we wrote to draw the light gray grid on the background. It uses two for-loops, one for the horizontal lines, and one for the vertical lines. We've also learned some new Processing functions to draw the most basic shapes. Let's take a look at what they do.

- The `rect()` function can be used with four, five, or eight parameters. The one with four parameters is the most common, and is used to draw a normal rectangle. The first two parameters are the x and y coordinates, the third and fourth parameters are the width and height of the rectangle. If you want to draw a square, you need to use the `rect()` function, and use the same value for the width and height, as Processing doesn't have a `square()` function. The `rect()` function with five or eight parameters is new in Processing 2, and is used for drawing rounded rectangles. If you use the `rect()` function with five parameters, the fifth parameter is used to set the radius for the rounded corners. The `rect()` function with eight parameters is used to set a radius for each corner, starting with the upper left corner, going clockwise for the other corners.

- The `ellipse()` function is similar to the `rect()` function, as it uses the first two parameters for the location, and the last two for the width and height. Note that the ellipse is drawn from the center. If you want to draw a circle, you can use the `ellipse()` function with the same value for the width and height. There is no `circle()` function in Processing.

- The `triangle()` function is used with six parameters. These are three x/y coordinates for the three points of the triangle. You should try to draw these points clockwise on the screen to keep things simple.

- The `quad()` is similar to the `triangle()` function, but uses eight parameters, as a quad has four points.

Working with colors

Color can be a great way to make your artwork more interesting. If you've used tools such as Photoshop before, you may know that there are different systems to describe a color. There is CMYK, LAB, HSB, HSV, RGB, XYZ, and so on. In Processing, you can use the RGB and HSB color modes to change the background, or set the fill or stroke of a shape. In this recipe, we'll explore how you can do this.

How to do it...

The first thing we'll do is declare a color variable named c, right before the setup() function. We'll set its value to a random color.

```
color c;

void setup()
{
  size( 640, 480 );
  smooth();

  c = color( random( 255 ), random( 255 ), random( 255 ) );
}
```

The second thing we'll do is to draw a rectangle with a gradient from black to white. This piece of code draws 255 rectangles, each with a different fill. This is the first piece of code that goes inside the draw() function.

```
Void draw()
{
  colorMode( RGB, 255 );
  background( 255 );

  // grayscale
  noStroke();
  for ( int i = 0; i < 255; i++ ) {
    fill( i );
    rect( i * 2 + 20, 20, 2, 120 );
  }

  stroke( 0 );
  noFill();
  rect( 20, 20, 500, 120 );
}
```

Next up is drawing a rectangle next to the grayscale gradient, filled with our random color. This should be added at the end of the draw() function.

```
// random color
fill( c );
stroke( 0 );
rect( 540, 20, 80, 120 );
```

Below our gradient and random color rectangles, we'll draw a series of swatches that will remind you of the test cards used on televisions. The colors we'll use are red, green, blue, cyan, magenta, yellow, white, and black. Add this to the end of the `draw()` function:

```
// full opaque colors
stroke( 0 );
fill( 255, 0, 0 );
rect( 20, 160, 75, 60 );
fill( 0, 255, 0 );
rect( 95, 160, 75, 60 );
fill( 0, 0, 255 );
rect( 170, 160, 75, 60 );
fill( 0, 255, 255 );
rect( 245, 160, 75, 60 );
fill( 255, 0, 255 );
rect( 320, 160, 75, 60 );
fill( 255, 255, 0 );
rect( 395, 160, 75, 60 );
fill( 255 );
rect( 470, 160, 75, 60 );
fill( 0 );
rect( 545, 160, 75, 60 );
```

For the second row of the test card, we'll use transparent versions of the colors we've used in the first row. You'll also draw a black rectangle behind those swatches. The transparency of the swatches is controlled with the mouse. This should be added to the end of the `draw()` function.

```
// black background behind transparent colors
rect( 0, 250, width, 70 );

float t = map( mouseX, 0, width, 0, 255 );

// transparent colors
fill( 255, 0, 0, t );
rect( 20, 220, 75, 60 );
fill( 0, 255, 0, t );
rect( 95, 220, 75, 60 );
fill( 0, 0, 255, t );
rect( 170, 220, 75, 60 );
fill( 0, 255, 255, t );
rect( 245, 220, 75, 60 );
fill( 255, 0, 255, t );
rect( 320, 220, 75, 60 );
fill( 255, 255, 0, t );
rect( 395, 220, 75, 60 );
fill( 255, t );
rect( 470, 220, 75, 60 );
fill( 0, t );
rect( 545, 220, 75, 60 );
```

This is the last piece of code we'll add to the `draw()` function. We will switch to the HSB color mode. The following code will draw a gradient from black to a color. The hue of the color is defined by the x position of your mouse, the saturation is defined by the y position.

```
// HSB color bar
colorMode( HSB, 360, 100, 100, 100 );

float h = map( mouseX, 0, width, 0, 360 );
float s = map( mouseY, 0, height, 0, 100 );

noStroke();
for ( int i = 0; i < 100; i++ ) {
  fill( h, s, i );
  rect( 20 + i*6, 340, 6, 120 );
}

noFill();
stroke(0);
rect( 20, 340, 600, 120 );
```

If you run the example, you'll see the test screen as shown in the following screenshot with grayscale, RGB, and HSB colors:

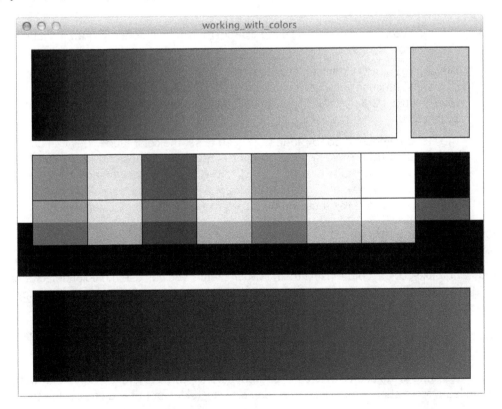

How it works...

The functions we've used in this example are similar to each other. `color()`, `stroke()`, and `fill()` can be used with the same parameters. If you use only one parameter, for these functions, you will work in grayscale. The default color mode in Processing is RGB and takes values between 0 and 255. So `color(0)` is used for black, and `color(255)` is used for white. Anything between these values will give you a gray color. If you use any of these functions with two parameters, the second one will be used for the transparency of the color. If you use three parameters, they will be used for the red, green, and blue components of the color. Adding a fourth parameter will result in a transparent color.

- The `color()` function is used to create a variable of the type color. This is handy if you need to create colors you can use anywhere in your sketch. In this example, I've declared a color variable named **c**, before the `setup()` function.

- The `fill()` function is used to set the fill color of the shape you're about to draw. It can be used with one to four parameters. You can also use a color variable for this.

- The `noFill()` function is used to disable the fill before you draw a shape to the screen.

- The `stroke()` is similar to the `fill()` function, but sets the color for the stroke of the shape you want to draw.

- The `noStroke()` function is used to disable the stroke before you draw a shape to the screen.

- The `background()` function is used to set the background color. This will usually be the first function you'll use inside the `draw()` function, as it will clear the screen. You can't use transparent colors with this function. If you do, the alpha value will be ignored.

- The first parameter in `colorMode()` is used to set the color mode. This can be either RGB or HSB. The default color mode is RGB, with values between 0 and 255. You can use `colorMode( RGB, 1.0 )` to use values between 0 and 1 for the color components. If you want to use HSB colors, you'll usually use `colorMode( HSB, 360, 100, 100 )`, as these numbers are used in most graphics applications.

There's more...

If you want to pick colors before using them in your sketch, you can use the color selector tool that is included with Processing. Go to the **Tools | Color Selector** menu to open this handy little app.

See also

The `background()` function can use transparent colors if you use it for off-screen drawing. You can learn more about that in the *Off-screen drawing* recipe at the end of this chapter.

Working with images

In the previous recipes, we've drawn vector-based shapes to the screen. Processing can also be used to manipulate images. In this recipe, we'll take a look at loading an image, displaying it on the screen, changing the color of a pixel, and copy/paste parts of an image.

Getting ready

Open one of your favorite pictures, resize and crop it with Photoshop so it's 640 x 480 pixels. If you don't have Photoshop, you can use GIMP, an open source image editor. GIMP is available for Linux, Windows, and Mac OS X. You can get it at http://www.gimp.org/.

How to do it...

Create a new sketch and save it as working_with_images.pde. Once you have done this, you can drag the picture you've just resized onto the Processing editor. This is the easiest way to add files to your sketch. If you've completed these steps, you can start typing code. The first thing we'll do is declare some variables.

```
PImage img;

// some settings to play with
boolean pixelMode = false;
int copyWidth = 50;
int copyHeight = 3;
```

Inside the setup() function, you'll set the size of the window, and load the image you've saved to the data folder into the PImage object:

```
void setup()
{
  size( 640, 480 );
  smooth();

  img = loadImage("osaka-fluo.jpg");
}
```

In the draw() function, we'll calculate some random numbers that will be used to swap pixels or areas of the image. The if-else part is the pixel-swapping algorithm. Finally, we'll draw the new image to the screen using the image() function.

```
void draw()
{
  int x1 = floor( random( width ) );
  int y1 = floor( random( height ) );
```

```
    int x2 = floor( random( width ) );
    int y2 = floor( random( height ) );

    if ( pixelMode == true ) {
      color c1 = img.get( x1, y1 );
      color c2 = img.get( x2, y2 );
      img.set( x1, y1, c2 );
      img.set( x2, y2, c1 );
    } else {
      PImage crop1 = img.get( x1, y1, copyWidth, copyHeight );
      PImage crop2 = img.get( x2, y2, copyWidth, copyHeight );
      img.set( x1, y1, crop2 );
      img.set( x2, y2, crop1 );
    }

    image( img, 0, 0 );
  }
```

The following screenshot shows you what the result will look like with the default values for the variables:

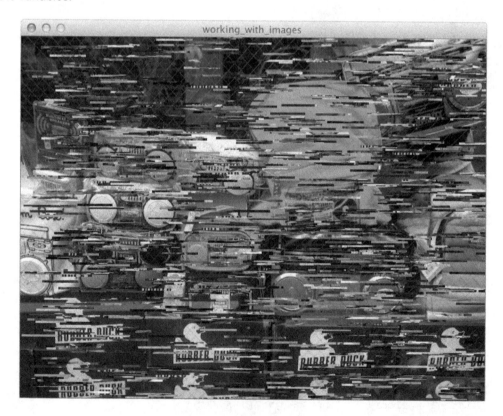

How it works...

When you dragged the image onto the editor, Processing made a copy of that file and stored it in the `data` folder of your sketch. You can see this folder by going to the **Sketch | Show Sketch Folder** menu.

Before you can use an image in Processing, you need to declare a `PImage` object. The `loadImage()` function is used in the `setup()` function to load the image from the data folder in the `PImage` object.

To copy pixels, or change their colors, you'll be using the `get()` and `set()` methods of the `PImage` class. These can be used with two or four parameters. If you use the `get()` method with two parameters, it will return the color for that specific coordinate. If you use it with four parameters, it will return a `PImage` object. The first two parameters are used to define the x/y coordinates for the upper-left corner, the third and fourth set the width and height of the region of pixels you want to copy. The `set()` method is similar to get, but is used to change the color of a single pixel or rectangular area of pixels.

In the example, I've used a boolean variable called `pixelMode` to switch between changing single pixels or areas of pixels. The `copyWidth` and `copyHeight` variables are used to define the size of the region of pixels you want to copy/paste.

There's more...

Use the things you've learned in the *Responding to keyboard events* recipe in *Chapter 1, Getting Started with Processing 2*, to create an interface so that you can change the parameters on the fly. This might be interesting to create a different kind of artwork.

Drawing text

If you are used to doing typesetting in applications such as InDesign, you'll know that you have a lot of control over things such as kerning and hyphenation. In Processing, this won't be the case. The things you can do with typography are somewhat limited, but you can still do quite a lot.

Getting ready

To get started, you'll need some fonts to work with. I've used Ostrich Sans and Junction, both open source fonts by The League of Moveable Type. You can download them at `http://www.theleagueofmoveabletype.com`. After downloading these fonts, you need to install them on your machine, so they are available to use.

To use fonts in Processing, you need to convert them from their original file format to the `.vlw` file format Processing uses. You can do this with the **Create Font** tool. Select the font you need, set a size, and click on the **OK** button. The `.vlw` font will be saved to the data folder of your sketch.

How to do it...

We'll start by declaring two PFont objects, one for each font. Inside the setup() function, we'll use the loadFont() function to load the `.vlw` files into the PFont object:

```
PFont ostrichSans;
PFont junction;

void setup()
{
  size( 640, 480 );
```

```
    smooth();

    ostrichSans = loadFont("OstrichSans-Bold-48.vlw");
    junction = loadFont("Junction-24.vlw");

    strokeCap( SQUARE );
}
```

The first thing we'll do is draw two lines of text, each in a different font. The following code goes inside the `draw()` function:

```
Void draw()
{
    background( 255 );
    fill( 128, 0, 0 );
    textFont( ostrichSans, 48 );
    textAlign( LEFT );
    text( "Hello, I'm Ostrich Sans", 20, 50 );

    textFont( junction, 24 );
    text("I'm a line of text, set in Junction.", 20, 80);

    stroke( 128, 0, 0 );
    strokeWeight( 1 );
    line( 20, 94, 620, 94 );
    line( 20, 96, 620, 96 );
}
```

Processing can also resize the text you want to draw if you set the the second parameter of the `textFont()` function. The next piece of code will draw three lines of text set in Junction, each with different size. Add them to the end of the `draw()` function.

```
    fill( 0 );
    textFont( junction, 24 );
    text( "The quick brown fox jumps over the lazy dog. (24)", 20, 130 );
    textFont( junction, 18 );
    text( "Pack my box with five dozen liquor jugs. (18)", 20, 154 );
    textFont( junction, 12 );
    text( "Blowzy red vixens fight for a quick jump. (12)", 20, 172 );

    stroke( 128 );
    strokeWeight( 3 );
    line( 20, 186, 620, 186 );
```

In the next step, we'll draw a rectangle with a vertical line right in the middle. This line will be used to align three lines of text to the left-hand side, right-hand side, and center of it. Add these lines of code to the end of the `draw()` function.

```
fill( 245 );
stroke( 128 );
strokeWeight( 1 );
rect( 20, 192, 600, 110 );

stroke( 128 );
line( width/2, 192, width/2, 298 );

fill( 128 );
stroke( 128 );
triangle( width/2-4, 192, width/2+4, 192, width/2, 196 );
triangle( width/2-4, 302, width/2+4, 302, width/2, 298 );

fill( 0 );
textFont( junction, 24 );
textAlign( LEFT );
text( "since I left you", width/2, 225 );
textAlign( CENTER );
text( "symmetry is boring", width/2, 252 );
textAlign( RIGHT );
text( "flush to the right", width/2, 280 );
```

Processing can also handle blocks with multiple lines of text. You can even change the leading for each block of text you'll draw to the screen. This piece of code should be added to the end of the `draw()` function.

```
textFont( junction, 14 );
textAlign( LEFT );
String multiline = "In typography, leading refers\n";
multiline += "to the distance between the\n";
multiline += "baselines of successive lines\n";
multiline += "of type.";

float standardLeading = ( textAscent() + textDescent() ) * 1.275f;

textLeading( standardLeading );
text( multiline, 20, 340 );
textLeading( standardLeading * 0.75 );
text( multiline, 220, 340 );
textLeading( standardLeading * 1.5 );
text( multiline, 420, 340 );
```

In the last piece of code we'll add to the draw() function, we'll use the textWidth() function to calculate the width of a line of text. We'll use the calculated value to draw a line below the text.

```
textFont( ostrichSans, 36 );
String s = "textWidth";
float w = textWidth( s );
fill( 128, 0, 0 );
text( s, 20, 450 );
noStroke();
rect( 20, 455, w, 8 );
```

If you've used the same fonts, the result of your sketch should look as shown in the following screenshot:

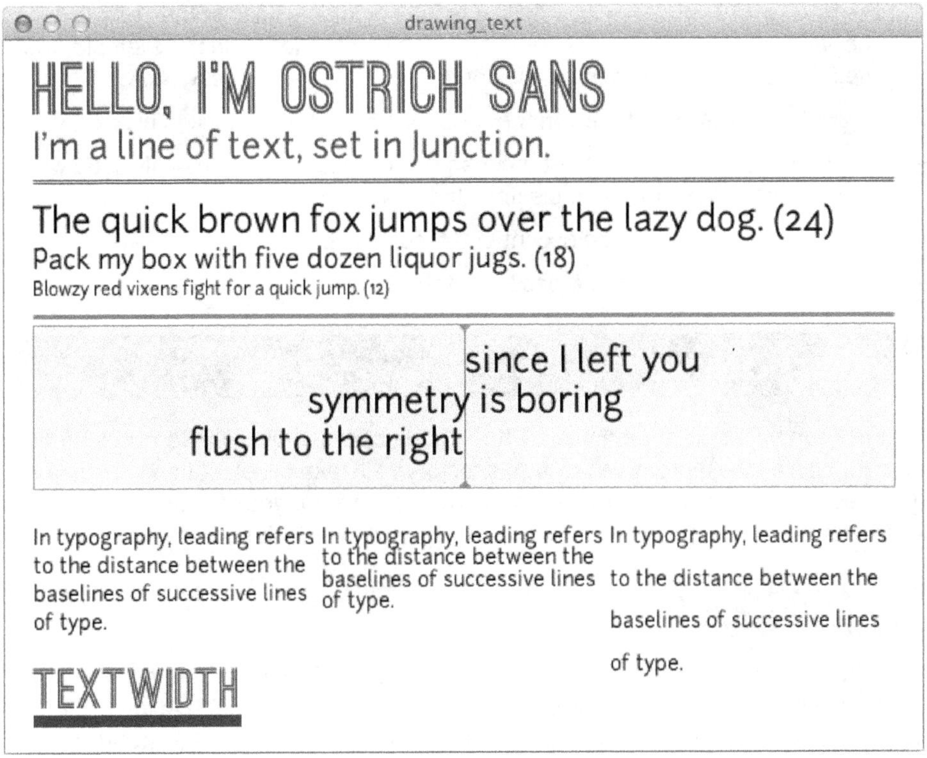

How it works...

You've learned everything there is to know about working with typography in Processing. Let's take a look at the functions we've used in this recipe:

- `text()` is used to draw text to the screen. The first parameter is usually a variable of the String type, but you can also use an array of char variables. The second and third parameters are the x and y coordinates of the location where you want to draw the text.

- `loadFont()` is used to load a font from the data folder of your sketch into a `PFont` variable. You'll need to create a font first using the **Create Font...** tool.

- `textFont()` is usually called right before `text()` and is used to set the font and the font size that will be used to draw the text to the screen.

- `textAlign()` is used to align the text to the coordinate used in the `text()` function. The value of the parameter can be `LEFT`, `RIGHT`, or `CENTER`. In the example, you've used this function to align three lines of text to the center of the window.

- `textWidth()` is used to return the width of a certain text block in pixels.

- `textLeading()` is used to set the leading of the text. This is usually used when you draw a block of text with multiple lines to the screen.

- `textAscent()` returns the ascent of the current font.

- `textDescent()` returns the descent of the font.

Drawing curves

Straight lines can be boring sometimes, so it might be useful to draw curved lines to make your artwork look a little more organic. In this recipe, we'll take a look at how you can draw Bézier curves and Catmull-Rom splines. If you have used vector graphics software such as Adobe Illustrator or Inkscape before, you might recognize the Bézier curves we'll draw.

How to do it...

The first thing we need to do is to import the OpenGL library. This library is usually used to draw in 3D. Although we won't be drawing in 3D in this example, we need to import it because the `bezierDetail()` and `curveDetail()` functions don't work with the standard 2D renderer. You can import the OpenGL library by going to the **Sketch | Import Library... | OpenGL**. Once you have done this, you can type the following code into the editor:

```
import processing.opengl.*;

void setup()
{
```

```
    size( 640, 480, OPENGL );
    smooth();
}
```

Inside the `draw()` function, we'll start with drawing some Bézier curves. The `bezierDetail()` function is used to change the appearance of the Bézier curves.

```
Void draw()
{
    background( 255 );

    noFill();

    for ( int i = 0; i < 15; i++ ) {
        pushMatrix();
        translate( (i * 40) + 20, 0 );
        bezierDetail( i + 4 );
        stroke( 0 );
        bezier( 0, 20, 50, 10, 80, 100, 30, 200 );
        stroke( 255, 0, 0, 128 );
        line( 0, 20, 50, 10 );
        line( 80, 100, 30, 200 );
        popMatrix();
    }
}
```

The next thing we'll do is draw some Catmull-Rom splines using the `curve()` function. The x coordinate of the mouse position is used to set the tightness of the curve. This piece of code should be added at the end of the `draw()` function.

```
float t = map( mouseX, 0, width, -5.0, 5.0 );
curveTightness( t );

for ( int i = 0; i < 15; i++ ) {
    pushMatrix();
    translate( (i * 40) + 20, 220 );
    curveDetail( i + 4 );
    stroke( 0 );
    curve( 10, 50, 0, 20, 30, 200, -50, 250 );
    stroke( 255, 0, 0, 128 );
    line( 10, 50, 0, 20 );
    line( 30, 200, -50, 250 );
    popMatrix();
}
```

The result of the sketch looks as shown in the following screenshot:

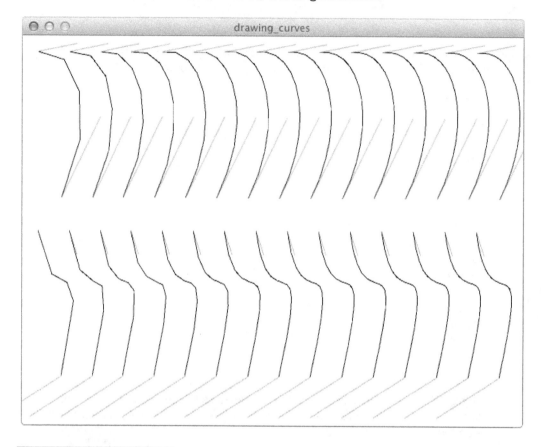

How it works...

We've used some new functions to draw different kinds of curves, and change their appearance. Let's take a look at how they work:

- ▸ bezier() draws a Bézier curve to the screen. The first two parameters are the coordinates for the first anchor point. The third and fourth parameters are the coordinates for the first control point. Parameters five and six are the coordinates for the second control point, and the last two parameters are the coordinates for the second anchor point.

- ▸ bezierDetail() sets the detail of the Bézier curve. The default value is 20.

- ▸ curve() draws a curve to the screen. This is a Processing implementation of Catmull-Rom splines. It works in a similar way to the bezier() function, but the coordinates for the anchor and control points are swapped.

- curveDetail() sets the detail level of the curve. This function is similar to the bezierDetail() function.
- curveTightness() sets the tightness of the curve. The default value is 0.0. If you want to connect the points with straight lines, you can use 1.0. You can use values between -5.0 and 5.0 to create a curve through the same points. Each of these values will give you a slightly different curve.

Calculating points on a curve

In the *Drawing curves* recipe, you've learned how to draw Bézier curves and Catmull-Rom splines. This example will teach you how you can use the bezierPoint() and curvePoint() functions to calculate points on those curves.

How to do it...

This is the code for the recipe. I've used the noise() function to animate the point as it moves along the curve. Mouse movement is used to animate the curve drawn with the curve() function.

```
float noiseOffset;

void setup()
{
  size( 640, 480 );
  smooth();

  noiseOffset = 0.0;

  rectMode( CENTER );
}

void draw()
{
  noiseOffset += 0.01;

  background( 255 );

  // Bézier curve
  stroke( 0 );
  noFill();
  bezier( 40, 200, 120, 40, 300, 240, 600, 40 );

  stroke( 255, 0, 0 );
```

```
line( 40, 200, 120, 40 );
line( 600, 40, 300, 240 );

fill( 255 );
rect( 120, 40, 4, 4 );
rect( 300, 240, 4, 4 );

float n = noise( noiseOffset );

float x = bezierPoint( 40, 120, 300, 600, n );
float y = bezierPoint( 200, 40, 240, 40, n );

stroke( 0 );
rect( x, y, 6, 6 );

float t = map( mouseX, 0, width, -5.0, 5.0 );
curveTightness( t );

// Catmull-Rom spline
stroke( 0 );
noFill();
curve( 120, 240, 40, 400, 600, 240, 300, 440 );

stroke( 255, 0, 0 );
line( 120, 240, 40, 400 );
line( 600, 240, 300, 440 );

fill( 255 );
rect( 120, 240, 4, 4 );
rect( 300, 440, 4, 4 );

x = curvePoint( 120, 40, 600, 300, n );
y = curvePoint( 240, 400, 240, 440, n );

stroke( 0 );
rect( x, y, 6, 6 );
}
```

The result of this sketch looks as shown in the following screenshot, move your mouse to see the interaction.

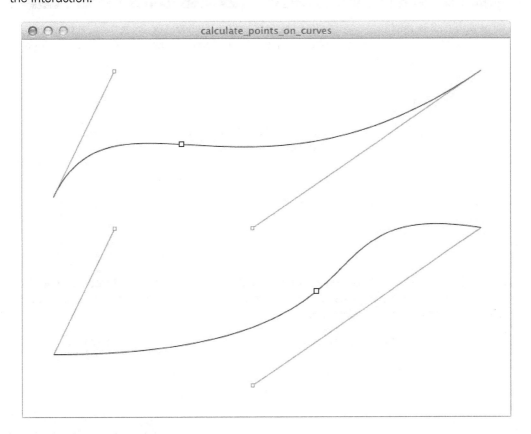

How it works...

You've learned some new functions to calculate points Bézier curves and Catmull-Rom splines. Let's take a deeper look at what these functions do.

► The `bezierPoint()` function takes five parameters. The first four take coordinates for the anchor and control points of the curve. The fifth parameter is a number between 0 and 1. I've used the `noise()` function to generate this number, as it returns numbers between 0 and 1. If the value of the fifth parameter is close to 0, the calculated point will be close to the first anchor point, if the value is close to 1, the point will be closer to the second anchor point. You need to use this function twice, once for the x coordinate and once for the y coordinate of the new point.

► The `curvePoint()` function works in a similar way to the `bezierPoint()` function. Take a good look at the code in the example to see which numbers correspond to each other.

Drawing custom shapes

Squares and circles might be boring after using them for a while. Luckily for you, Processing has some functions to draw custom shapes. We'll take a look at how you can write functions for drawing stars and flowers.

How to do it...

We'll start by writing the code for the `setup()` function. I've used the `frameRate()` function to make the sketch run at one frame per second.

```
void setup()
{
  size( 640, 480 );
  smooth();
  frameRate( 1 );
}
```

The next thing we'll do is write a function to draw a star. The function takes three parameters: an integer for the number of spikes on the star, and two float variables for the inner and outer radius we'll use to calculate the vertices.

```
void star( int numSpikes, float innerRadius, float outerRadius )
{
  int numVertices = numSpikes * 2;
  float angleStep = TWO_PI / numVertices;

  beginShape();
  for ( int i = 0; i < numVertices; i++ ) {
    float x, y;
    if ( i % 2 == 0 ) {
      x = cos( angleStep * i ) * outerRadius;
      y = sin( angleStep * i ) * outerRadius;
    } else {
      x = cos( angleStep * i ) * innerRadius;
      y = sin( angleStep * i ) * innerRadius;
    }
    vertex( x, y );
  }
  endShape( CLOSE );
}
```

The function to draw a flower is similar to the one for the star. The only difference is that we'll use the `bezierVertex()` function to draw the organic shape for the leaves of the flower.

```
void flower( int numLeafs, float innerRadius, float outerRadius )
{
  float angleStep = TWO_PI / numLeafs;

  beginShape();
  float startX = cos( 0 ) * innerRadius;
  float startY = sin( 0 ) * outerRadius;
  vertex( startX, startY );
  for ( int i = 0; i < numLeafs; i++ ) {
    float cx1 = cos( angleStep * i ) * outerRadius;
    float cy1 = sin( angleStep * i ) * outerRadius;
    float x2 = cos( angleStep * (i + 1) ) * innerRadius;
    float y2 = sin( angleStep * (i + 1) ) * innerRadius;
    float cx2 = cos( angleStep * (i + 1) ) * outerRadius;
    float cy2 = sin( angleStep * (i + 1) ) * outerRadius;
    bezierVertex( cx1, cy1, cx2, cy2, x2, y2 );
  }
  endShape( CLOSE );
}
```

Inside the `draw()` function, we'll use the `star()` and `flower()` functions we just wrote. In each frame, the sketch will draw 75 custom shapes. There's a 50 percent chance for each shape.

```
void draw()
{
  background( 0 );
  noStroke();

  for ( int i = 0; i < 75; i++ ) {
    int numPoints = floor( random( 4, 8 ) );
    float innerRadius = random( 20, 40 );
    float outerRadius = random( 50, 100 );

    pushMatrix();
    translate( random( width ), random( height ) );
    if ( random( 100 ) < 50 ) {
      fill( 255, 255, 0, 64 );
      star( numPoints, innerRadius, outerRadius );
    } else {
      fill( 255, 0, 0, 64 );
      flower( numPoints, innerRadius, outerRadius );
    }
    popMatrix();
  }
}
```

The result of the sketch will look somewhat as shown in the following screenshot:

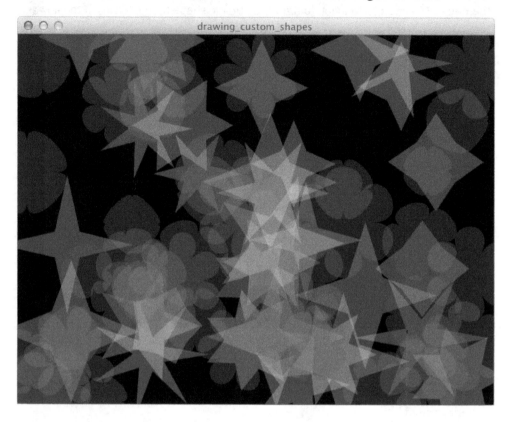

How it works...

The beginShape() function is used together with the endShape() function. If you want a closed shape, you need to add the CLOSE parameter to the endShape() function. These functions connect all vertices you add between them. If you use the vertex() function, these points will be connected with straight lines. The bezierVertex() and curveVertex() functions can be used to connect the points with a curve. They work just like the bezier() and curve() functions, but they only take six parameters. The first anchor point is left out, because the anchor point of the previous point will be used. Note that you'll need to use the vertex() function first before you can use bezierVertex() or curveVertex().

There's more...

Processing uses radians as the unit for angles. This might be a little confusing for people using the metric system. You can use degrees if you want to, but you'll have to convert them to radians if you want to calculate the sine or cosine. This can be done using the `radians()` function. If you want to convert radians to degrees, you can use the `degrees()` function. Processing also has some handy mathematical constants you can use when you are dealing with trigonometry. In our functions, we've used the `TWO_PI` constant, which represents the number of radians to create a full circle. The other constants that are available are `QUARTER_PI`, `THIRD_PI`, `HALF_PI`, and `PI`.

Manipulating SVG files

A great thing about Processing is that you don't always have to draw your own shapes. You can draw just about anything you want in a vector editing program, and export it as an SVG file to use in Processing.

Getting ready

The first thing you need to do is create an SVG file to use in your sketch. Processing supports SVG files made with Adobe Illustrator or Inkscape. Inkscape is an open source vector editor, so it might be useful if you don't have access to an expensive piece of software, such as Illustrator. You can download it at: `http://inkscape.org/`.

Create a new sketch and save it as `manipulating_svg_files.pde` in your sketchbook. Save your SVG file in the data folder of your sketch. You can do this by dragging the SVG file on the Processing editor, just like you did in the recipe on working with images.

How to do it...

We'll start with declaring some `PShape` objects and loading them inside the `setup()` function. The `snowFlake` variable is used to load your SVG file, the other variables will be used to store individual parts of the main SVG file.

```
PShape snowFlake;
PShape small1;
PShape small2;
PShape small3;
PShape small4;
PShape small5;
PShape small6;
PShape big1;

void setup()
```

```
{
  size( 640, 480 );
  smooth();

  snowFlake = loadShape("snowflake.svg");

  small1 = snowFlake.getChild("small1");
  small2 = snowFlake.getChild("small2");
  small3 = snowFlake.getChild("small3");
  small4 = snowFlake.getChild("small4");
  small5 = snowFlake.getChild("small5");
  small6 = snowFlake.getChild("small6");
  big1 = snowFlake.getChild("big1");

  shapeMode( CENTER );
}
```

Inside the `draw()` function, we'll draw the SVG files to the screen using the `shape()` function:

```
void draw()
{
  background( 255 );

  // regular snowflake
  shape( snowFlake, 160, 120 );

  // distorted snowflake
  shape( snowFlake, 480, 120, 160, 80 );

  // orange snowflake
  snowFlake.disableStyle();
  fill( 255, 128, 0 );
  stroke( 255 );
  strokeWeight( 2 );
  shape( snowFlake, 160, 360 );
  snowFlake.enableStyle();

  // draw separate parts (colorful star)
  strokeWeight( 1 );
  stroke( 0 );
  small1.disableStyle();
```

```
    fill( 151, 183, 189 );
    shape( small1, 480, 360 );
    small1.enableStyle();
    small2.disableStyle();
    fill( 216, 234, 237 );
    shape( small2, 480, 360 );
    small2.enableStyle();

    small3.disableStyle();
    fill( 151, 183, 189 );
    shape( small3, 480, 360 );
    small3.enableStyle();

    small4.disableStyle();
    fill( 216, 234, 237 );
    shape( small4, 480, 360 );
    small4.enableStyle();

    small5.disableStyle();
    fill( 151, 183, 189 );
    shape( small5, 480, 360 );
    small5.enableStyle();

    small6.disableStyle();
    fill( 108, 223, 234 );
    shape( small6, 480, 360 );
    small6.enableStyle();

    strokeWeight( 2 );
    big1.disableStyle();
    fill( 251, 0, 95 );
    stroke( 255 );
    shape( big1, 480, 360 );
    big1.enableStyle();
}
```

The result of this sketch will look somewhat as shown in the following screenshot:

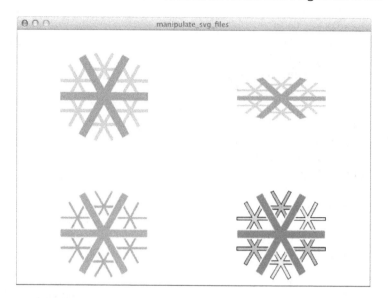

How it works...

An SVG file is basically an XML file. Try opening your drawing in your favorite text editor to see what it looks like.

```
1   <?xml version="1.0" encoding="utf-8"?>
2   <!-- Generator: Adobe Illustrator 13.0.0, SVG Export Plug-In . SVG Version: 6.(
3   <!DOCTYPE svg PUBLIC "-//W3C//DTD SVG 1.1//EN" "http://www.w3.org/Graphics/SVG,
4   <svg version="1.1" id="Layer_1" xmlns="http://www.w3.org/2000/svg" xmlns:xlink=
5       width="160px" height="160px" viewBox="0 0 160 160" enable-background="new
6   <path id="small4" inkscape:label="#path4000" inkscape:connector-curvature="0" 1
7       l13.504,23.386H48v5.769h27.007l-13.504,23.385l4.992,2.885L80,131.474l13.50
8       l13.504-23.386l-5-2.885L80,119.935L66.496,96.55z"/>
9   <path id="small1" inkscape:label="#path4002" inkscape:connector-curvature="0" 1
10      l13.504,23.384H48v5.769h27.007L61.503,55.422l4.992,2.884L80,34.922l13.504,;
11      L98.503,2.885l-5-2.884L80,23.385L66.496,0z"/>
12  <path id="small2" inkscape:label="#path3970" inkscape:connector-curvature="0" 1
13      l13.504,23.384H96v5.769h27.011-13.504,23.384l4.99,2.884L128,54.828l13.506,;
14      l13.504-23.384l-5-2.884L128,43.291l114.496,19.907L114.496,19.907z"/>
15  <path id="small3" inkscape:label="#path3996" inkscape:connector-curvature="0" 1
16      l13.504,23.384H96v5.77h27.011-13.504,23.385l4.99,2.885L128,107.335l13.506,;
17      l13.504-23.384l-5-2.884L128,95.796l114.496,72.413L114.496,72.413z"/>
18  <path id="small5" inkscape:label="#path3994" inkscape:connector-curvature="0" 1
19      l13.504,23.384H0v5.77h27.008l-13.504,23.385l4.991,2.885l13.504-23.385l13.5(
20      l13.504-23.384l-5.001-2.884L32,95.796L18.496,72.413z"/>
21  <path id="small6" inkscape:label="#path3998" inkscape:connector-curvature="0" 1
22      l13.504,23.384H0v5.769h27.008L13.504,75.328l4.991,2.884l13.504-23.384l13.5(
23      l13.504-23.384l-5.001-2.884L32,43.292L18.496,19.907z"/>
24  <path id="big1" inkscape:label="#rect3928" inkscape:connector-curvature="0" fil
25      l33.761,58.46H0v14.421h67.521l33.76,141.855l12.479,7.212L80,90.606l33.762,!
26      l33.762-58.46l-12.50z-7.211L80,61.762L46.239,3.302L46.239,3.302z"/>
27  </svg>
28
```

To load an SVG file into your sketch, you'll need to declare a `PShape` object before the `setup()` function. The next thing to do is to load the file into the object with the `loadShape()` function. You can draw the SVG file to the screen using the `shape()` function. The first parameter of this function is a reference to your `PShape` object, the second and third are the x and y coordinates where you want to draw the shape. You can add a fourth and fifth parameter to resize the shape if you want to. SVG files are normally drawn with their own styles, you can disable these styles with the `disableStyle()` method, and use the `fill()` and `stroke()` functions from Processing to change the colors of your PShape object. Make sure you use the `enableStyle()` method once you are finished. In the example, you've also used the `getChild()` method to access different shapes within the SVG file you've loaded. You need to use the text from the `id` attribute of the shape you want to get from the main SVG file. In our example, the line `small4 = snowFlake.getChild("small4");` gets the line of xml starting with `<path id="small4"` ....

There's more...

The full SVG specification however, is not implemented in Processing. Patterns for instance, will not work. So you might see an error message if your SVG file has properties that aren't supported in Processing.

Offscreen drawing

In some cases, you want to be able to draw things on a blank image, before drawing it to the screen. This can be easily done in Processing with the `PGraphics` object.

How to do it...

The first thing you need to do is declare a `PGraphics` object at the beginning of your sketch, and initialize it with the `createGraphics()` function inside `setup()`. I've added the x and y variable to add some animation to the sketch. You can clear the background by clicking the mouse.

```
PGraphics pg;

float x;
float y;

void setup()
{
  size( 640, 480 );
  smooth();
```

```
    pg = createGraphics( 64, 64, JAVA2D );

    background( 255 );
    imageMode( CENTER );

    x = 0;
    y = 0;
}
```

The first thing we'll do inside the `draw()` function is draw some lines onto the `PGraphics` object. The object will then be drawn to the screen using the `image()` function. The last piece of code inside the draw function is used to calculate the x and y values to animate the sketch.

```
void draw()
{
  pg.beginDraw();
  pg.background( 255, 0, 0, 8 );
  pg.smooth();
  for ( int i = 0; i < 8; i++ ) {
    pg.stroke( random( 255 ), 0, 0 );
    pg.line( random( pg.width ), random( pg.height ), random( pg.width
), random( pg.height ) );
  }
  pg.endDraw();

  image( pg, x, y );

  x += random( 4, 16 );
  if ( x > width ) {
    x = 0;
    y += random( 32, 64 );
    if ( y > height ) {
      y = 0;
      fill( 255, 32 );
      noStroke();
      rect( 0, 0, width, height );
    }
  }
}
```

The `mousePressed()` function is used to clear the screen. There's a 50 percent chance the new background will be black or white.

```
void mousePressed()
{
  if ( random( 100 ) < 50 ) {
```

```
    background( 0 );
  } else {
    background( 255 );
  }
}
```

The result of the sketch will look as shown in the following screenshot. Press the mouse to see what happens.

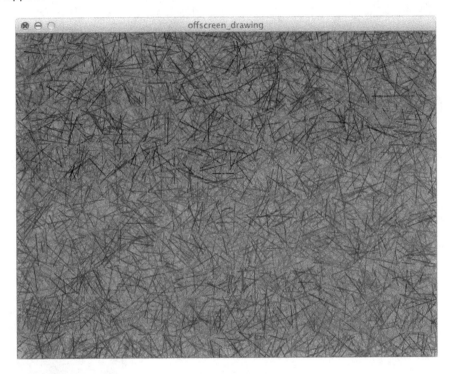

How it works...

The `createGraphics()` function creates the context you can draw on. Think of it as creating a new transparent image. The first two parameters are the width and height of the image, the third one is the renderer. I've used the P2D renderer since I'll draw some 2D lines on the image. To start drawing on the PGraphics object, you need to start with `pg.beginDraw()`. To stop drawing on the image you'll finish with `pg.endDraw()`. Anything between those lines will be drawn on the object. All drawing functions from Processing are available, but you'll need to prefix them with the name of your variable. So if you want to draw a line on your `PGraphics` object, you need to use `pg.line()`, for drawing rectangles, you'll use `pg.rect()`, and so on for all other functions. You can use `pg.width` and `pg.height` to get the width and height of your object. Note that I've used a transparent color for the `background()` function. This only works with the `PGraphics` object.

There's more...

If you need to draw a large amount of text, let's say a thousand words, you'll find that this can slow your sketch down. You can fix this by drawing those words, each on a different `PGraphics` object, in the `setup()` function. You can then draw those `PGraphics` objects to the screen with the `image()` function, which will speed things up.

3

Drawing in 3D–Lights, Camera, and Action!

In this chapter we will cover:

- ▸ Understanding 3D space
- ▸ Drawing 3D primitives
- ▸ Using lights
- ▸ Making polygon soup
- ▸ Mixing 2D and 3D objects
- ▸ Drawing triangle and quad strips
- ▸ Using textures
- ▸ Using the 3D camera

Introduction

In *Chapter 2*, *Drawing Text, Curves, and Shapes in 2D*, you learned about drawing shapes and text in a 2D environment. This chapter will teach you the basics of drawing in a 3D world. We'll start by taking a look at how the 3D environment is structured and how you can draw some basic 3D primitives. By the end of this chapter, you will also be able to use lights and textures to add more character to your 3D artwork.

Understanding 3D space

In *Chapter 1*, *Getting Started with Processing 2*, you learned about the coordinate system in Processing. In this recipe, we'll take a look at the third dimension, and draw objects in a 3D space.

How to do it...

The first thing you'll need to do is to import the OpenGL library. This will enable you to use the third dimension. You've done this before in the *Drawing curves* recipe, in *Chapter 2, Drawing Text, Curves, and Shapes in 2D*. Go to **Sketch | Import Library | OpenGL** to import the library using the following code:

```
import processing.opengl.*;
```

The next thing we need to do is declare two variables, right before the `setup()` function, and give them some values. Note that the `size()` function is a little different from the examples in *Chapter 2*.

```
float depth;
float zSpeed;

void setup()
{
  size( 640, 480, OPENGL );

  depth = 0;
  zSpeed = -1;
}
```

The first thing we'll do inside `draw()` is change the value of the `depth` variable, so we can use it for animation. The following piece of code will change the value, so it goes from 0 to 1000 and back again.

```
void draw()
{
  depth += zSpeed;

  if ( depth <= -1000 || depth >= 0 ) {
    zSpeed *= -1;
  }
}
```

The next thing we'll do is clear the background and draw some rectangles in 3D space. These rectangles don't have a fill color, only a border. Add the following piece of code at the end of the `draw()` function.

```
background( 255 );

noFill();
stroke( 0 );
for ( int i = 0; i < 10; i++ ) {
  pushMatrix();
```

```
    translate( 0, 0, -i * 100 );
    rect( 0, 0, width, height );
    popMatrix();
}
```

The last piece of code inside the `draw()` function is the following one. We'll basically draw four squares, one in each corner of the window. Each one has a different color.

```
pushMatrix();
translate( 0, 0, depth );
fill( 255, 0, 0 );
rect( 0, 0, 80, 80 );
fill( 0, 255, 0 );
rect( width-80, 0, 80, 80 );
fill( 255, 255, 0 );
rect( width-80, height-80, 80, 80 );
fill( 0, 255, 255 );
rect( 0, height-80, 80, 80 );
popMatrix();
```

If you run the example, you'll see the four colored rectangles move away and come closer again.

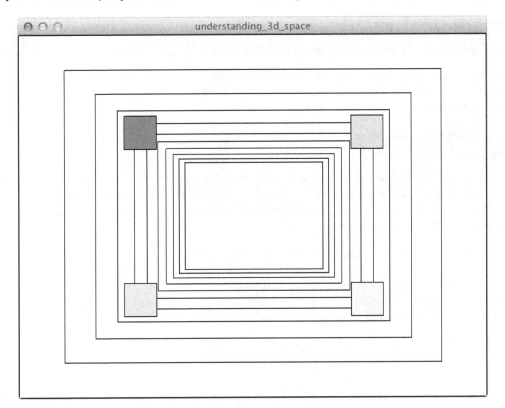

How it works...

To enable 3D in Processing, you'll need to add a third parameter to the `size()` function, to set the renderer. In this case, the parameter will be `OPENGL`. Don't forget to import the OpenGL library, or the sketch won't run.

In the previous chapter, you may have noticed that functions such as `rect()` and `ellipse()` only take *x* and *y* coordinates. There is no *z* coordinate to draw the shapes in a 3D environment. If you want to draw these flat 2D shapes in 3D, you'll need to make changes to the coordinate system using the `translate()` function. I've wrapped the blocks where I use the `translate()` function between `pushMatrix()` and `popMatrix()`.

The `pushMatrix()` function saves the current coordinate system. It is always used in combination with the `popMatrix()` function, which restores the coordinate system saved by the `pushMatrix()` function.

The `translate()` function uses three parameters when you use it in a 3D environment. These parameters are the *x*, *y*, and *z* coordinates for the new point of origin you will use. We've used the depth variable for the *z* coordinate of the `translate()` function, to animate the colored squares. Take a closer look at the red square while your sketch is running: it is always drawn at (0, 0), yet it doesn't look that way, because we move the point of origin in z-space.

Drawing 3D primitives

In the previous chapter, you learned about drawing basic 2D shapes. Processing also has some 3D primitives, by default—a box and a sphere. In this recipe, we'll take a look at how you can draw them.

How to do it...

I'm not going to write the code for the `setup()` function, in this recipe. You probably know, by now, how to use it. Import the OpenGL library, just as you did in the *Understanding 3D space* recipe and create a window with a resolution of 640 x 480 pixels. Don't forget to add the `OPENGL` parameter to the `size()` function.

Add the following piece of code to the `draw()` function. We reuse the `pushMatrix()`, `popMatrix()`, and `translate()` functions from the previous example. We are going to add the `rotateY()` function to rotate our 3D primitives. These primitives are drawn to the screen with the `box()` and `sphere()` functions. The `sphereDetail()` function is used to manipulate the shape of the sphere.

```
background( 255 );
lights();
```

```
float angleY = radians( frameCount );

pushMatrix();
translate( width * 0.3, height* 0.3 );
rotateY( angleY );
fill( 0, 255, 255 );
box( 100 );
popMatrix();

pushMatrix();
translate( width * 0.5, height* 0.5 );
rotateY( angleY );
fill( 0, 255, 0 );
box( 100, 40, 50 );
popMatrix();

pushMatrix();
translate( width * 0.7, height * 0.3 );
rotateY( angleY );
fill( 255, 0, 0 );
sphereDetail( 30 );
sphere( 75 );
popMatrix();

pushMatrix();
translate( width * 0.3, height * 0.7 );
rotateY( angleY );
fill( 255, 255, 0 );
sphereDetail( 6 );
sphere( 75 );
popMatrix();

pushMatrix();
translate( width * 0.7, height * 0.7 );
rotateY( angleY );
fill( 255, 0, 255 );
sphereDetail( 4, 20 );
sphere( 75 );
popMatrix();
```

After you've added this code to the `draw()` function, you can run the sketch. The result should look like the following screenshot:

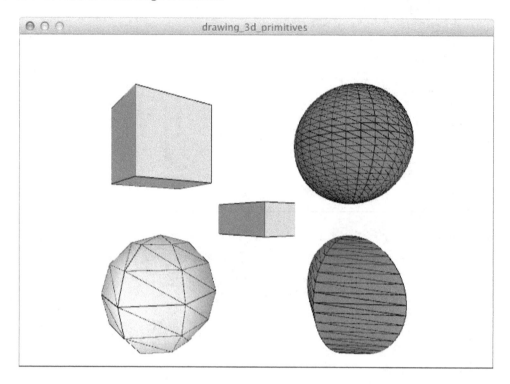

How it works...

The `box()` function can be used with one or three parameters. If you use it with only one parameter, you'll create a cube. Using the function with three parameters allows you to set different values for the width, depth, and height of the box.

The `sphere()` function only takes one parameter: the radius of the sphere. You can change the appearance of the sphere by using the `sphereDetail()` function before you call the `sphere()` function. The default sphere is quite detailed and has a resolution of 30. If you use a number lower than 30, the sphere will be less detailed; if you use a higher number, you'll add more detail. Using two parameters with this function, you can set the horizontal and vertical resolution of the sphere. If you use a low number for the first one and a higher number for the second one, you'll get a totally different kind of sphere.

There's more...

In the beginning of the `draw()` function, we've created a variable named `angleY`. This variable is used to rotate each 3D object around its Y-axis. In each frame, the objects will be rotated by one degree. We've used the `frameCount` system variable to do this, as the value of this variable is increased by 1 in each frame. We converted this value to radians, because Processing uses radians as the measurement unit for angles.

Using lights

If you want to make your 3D scene a little more interesting, you can add light, so your objects don't look flat. There are different kinds of lights available in Processing. We'll take a look at how you can use them in this recipe.

How to do it...

The first thing you need to do is import the OpenGL library and set up an OpenGL window with a resolution of 640 x 480 pixels. Before the `setup()` function, you need to declare two integers, `lightMode` and `lightDirection`, which will be used to switch between the different types of lighting. I've assigned these variables a value of 0 inside the `setup()` function.

```
lightMode = 0;
lightDirection = 0;
```

In the first block of code that goes inside the `draw()` function, we'll configure the different lights. The `lightMode` variable is used to switch between lights, and the `lightDirection` variable is used to set the direction when we are using directional lighting.

```
background( 0 );

switch ( lightMode ) {
  case 0:
    noLights();
    break;
  case 1:
    lights();
    break;
  case 2:
    if ( lightDirection == 0 ) {
      directionalLight( 255, 128, 0, 0, -1, 0 ); // UP
    } else if ( lightDirection == 1 ) {
      directionalLight( 0, 255, 0, 1, 0, 0 ); // RIGHT
    } else if ( lightDirection == 2 ) {
      directionalLight( 255, 0, 255, 0, 1, 0 ); // DOWN
```

```
    } else if ( lightDirection == 3 ) {
      directionalLight( 0, 255, 255, -1, 0, 0 ); // LEFT
    }
    break;
  case 3:
    ambientLight( 0, 255, 255 );
    break;
  case 4:
    pointLight( 255, 255, 0, 100, height*0.3, 100 );
    break;
  case 5:
    spotLight( 128, 255, 128, 800, 20, 300, -1, .25, 0, PI,
                 2 );
    break;
  default:
    noLights();
}
```

After you've set the lights, it's time to draw some 3D geometry. I've drawn a cube and a sphere at the same coordinates and have used the `rotateY()` and `rotateX()` functions to let them rotate in a different way.

```
pushMatrix();
translate( width/2, height/2, 0 );

pushMatrix();
rotateY( radians( frameCount ) );
fill( 255 );
noStroke();
sphere( 100 );
popMatrix();

pushMatrix();
rotateZ( radians( frameCount ) );
rotateX( radians( frameCount/2 ) );
fill( 255 );
noStroke();
box( 150 );
popMatrix();

popMatrix();
```

The last thing you need to do is to build some kind of keyboard interface to switch between the different light modes. The following code will allow you to do this. If you want to know how this works, read the *Responding to keyboard events* recipe, in *Chapter 1, Getting Started with Processing 2*.

```
void keyPressed()
{
  switch ( key ) {
    case 'n':
      lightMode = 0; // no lights
      break;
    case 'l':
      lightMode = 1; // lights
      break;
    case 'd':
      lightMode = 2; // directional light
      break;
    case 'a':
      lightMode = 3; // ambient light
      break;
    case 'p':
      lightMode = 4; // point light
      break;
    case 's':
      lightMode = 5; // spot light
      break;
  }

  if ( key == CODED ) {
    switch ( keyCode ) {
      case UP:
        lightDirection = 0;
        break;
      case RIGHT:
        lightDirection = 1;
        break;
      case DOWN:
        lightDirection = 2;
        break;
      case LEFT:
        lightDirection = 3;
        break;
    }
  }
}
```

When you have finished typing, you can use the *N, L, D, A, P*, and *S* keys to switch between the different light modes. The arrow keys can be used to change the direction of the light when directional light is used.

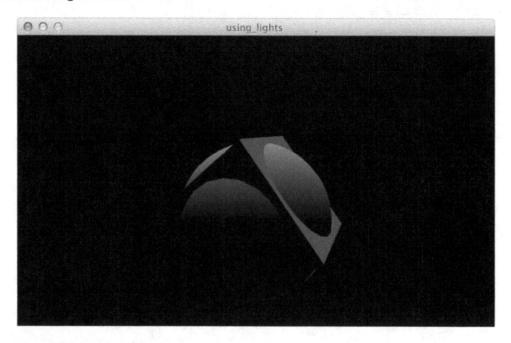

How it works...

The `lights()` function is the easiest one to use. It just enables the default lighting used in Processing. You can use the `noLights()` function to disable lighting. The `noLights()` function is the first thing you'll see when you run the sketch.

The `directionalLight()` function is used to send light from one direction. These lights are placed far away and affect everything in the scene. Think of this light as the sun. The first three parameters are the *r, g*, and *b* values for the color of the light. The last three parameters are used to set the direction of the light along the *x, y*, and *z* axes of your 3D scene. You can use values between -1 and 1 for these parameters.

The `ambientLight()` function is used to set the ambient light for your 3D scene. This light comes from just about every direction. You'll usually use this function together with other types of lights. You can use this function with three parameters to set the *r, g*, and *b* components for the color of the light. You also have the option to add a location in 3D space for the ambient light, if you use the function with six parameters.

The `pointLight()` function is similar to a light bulb. It shines equally in all directions. The first three parameters are used to set the color, while the last three parameters are the *x, y*, and *z* coordinates for the light in 3D space.

The spotLight() function is probably the hardest one to use. You need to use eleven parameters. The first block of three parameters is used for the color, the second block of three parameters consists of the *x*, *y*, and *z* coordinates for the light. Parameters 7, 8, and 9 are used to set the direction along the *x*, *y*, and *z* axes, just as you did with the directionalLight() function. The tenth parameter is used to set the angle of the light cone. Note that you need to set this angle in radians. The last parameter sets the concentration.

Making polygon soup

In the *Drawing 3D primitives* recipe, you've learned that Processing comes with two 3D primitives: the box and the sphere. Although these two shapes can be used to do great things, you might have more fun creating your own 3D shapes. We'll take a look at how you can create a flexible function to draw a cylinder in this recipe.

How to do it...

Just like in the previous recipes, you should start by importing the OpenGL library and setting up a window with a size of 640 x 480 pixels. The next thing we'll do is to write a function that will draw a cylinder to the screen. The code for the top and bottom of the cylinder should look familiar; we've used something similar in the *Drawing custom shapes* recipe, in the previous chapter. The code for the side of the cylinder is a little different.

```
void cylinder( int numSegments, float h, float r )
{
  float angle = 360.0 / (float)numSegments;

  // top
  beginShape();
  for ( int i = 0; i < numSegments; i++ ) {
    float x = cos( radians( angle * i ) ) * r;
    float y = sin( radians( angle * i ) ) * r;
    vertex( x, y, -h/2 );
  }
  endShape( CLOSE );

  // side
  beginShape( QUAD_STRIP );
  for ( int i = 0; i < numSegments + 1; i++ ) {
    float x = cos( radians( angle * i ) ) * r;
    float y = sin( radians( angle * i ) ) * r;
    vertex( x, y, -h/2 );
    vertex( x, y, h/2 );
  }
```

```
        endShape();

        // bottom
        beginShape();
        for ( int i = 0; i < numSegments; i++ ) {
          float x = cos( radians( angle * i ) ) * r;
          float y = sin( radians( angle * i ) ) * r;
          vertex( x, y, h/2 );
        }
        endShape( CLOSE );
    }
```

Now that we have a flexible function, it's time to use it and draw some cylinders to the screen. Type the following code inside the draw() function:

```
background( 255 );

pushMatrix();
translate( width*.3, height*.3, 0 );
rotateY( radians( frameCount ) );
fill( 255, 0, 0 );
cylinder( 30, 100, 50 );
popMatrix();

pushMatrix();
translate( width*.7, height*.5, 0 );
rotateY( radians( frameCount ) );
fill( 255, 255, 0 );
cylinder( 4, 200, 50 );
popMatrix();

pushMatrix();
translate( width*.3, height*.7, 0 );
rotateY( radians( frameCount ) );
fill( 0, 0, 255 );
cylinder( 3, 200, 30 );
popMatrix();
```

If everything goes well, the result of your sketch should look like the following screenshot. You can play around with the parameters of the `cylinder()` function to create a variety of different cylinders.

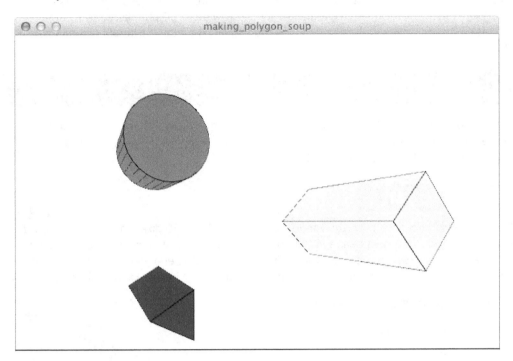

How it works...

Polygon soup is usually referred to as a collection of triangles with no particular order. The object might look like a real 3D object, but if you were to export this to print, on a 3D printer for instance, it would fail to print. This is however the easiest way to quickly draw things in a 3D environment.

Our cylinder doesn't have a data structure. The side of the cylinder shares vertices with the top and bottom, but these vertices are calculated twice. Ideally, you should have an array that keeps track of the vertices, and one that keeps track of how they are connected to each other.

The only new thing in this example is the use of the `QUAD_STRIP` parameter in the `beginShape()` function. This connects the vertices in a different way. You'll learn more about this in the *Drawing triangle and quad strips* recipe, later in this chapter.

There's more...

If you want to draw 3D objects with a decent data structure, you can use the Hemesh library by Frederik Vanhoutte. This will allow you to draw more 3D primitives, and create complex 3D objects without having to do too much difficult math. The library is available at http://hemesh.wblut.com/.

Mixing 2D and 3D objects

On some occasions, you'll want to draw 2D objects on top of your 3D environment. In this recipe, we'll take a look at how you can do this. This will be handy if you want to draw an interface or some text on top of everything.

How to do it...

The first thing to do is to set up an OpenGL window of 640 x 480 pixels. You should know this by now, since you've done it before in the previous recipes. You should also declare a float variable named n. We'll be using this variable to calculate 3D perlin noise for animating the size of the cubes in our 3D world. The first part of your sketch looks like the following:

```
import processing.opengl.*;

float n;

void setup()
{
  size( 640, 480, OPENGL );
  n = 0.0f;
}
```

The next thing we'll do is drawing a grid of cubes. We'll change the value of the n variable by adding 0.01 to each frame, so we get a different noise value for each cube. Type the following code inside the draw() function and run it to see what happens.

```
hint( ENABLE_DEPTH_TEST );
n += 0.01;

background( 255 );
lights();

noStroke();
fill( 255, 128, 0 );

pushMatrix();
for ( int i = 0; i < 17; i++ ) {
  for ( int j = 0; j < 13; j++ ) {
    pushMatrix();
    fill( i * 15, 0, j * 19 );
```

```
    translate( i * 40, j * 40 );
    rotateY( radians( i * 10 + frameCount ) );
    rotateZ( radians( i * 10 + frameCount ) );
    box( noise( i, j, n ) * 40 );
    popMatrix();
  }
}
popMatrix();
```

The last piece of code we need to add inside the `draw()` function is needed to draw some rectangles. Both rectangles will be drawn at the same *z* coordinate. The first one will intersect with the cubes, and the second one will be drawn on top of the 3D environment, hiding the cubes below.

```
noLights();

fill( 0 );
stroke( 0 );
rect( 320, 40, 200, 200 );

hint( DISABLE_DEPTH_TEST );
fill( 255 );
rect( 320, 240, 200, 200 );
```

Running the sketch will give you the result shown in the following screenshot. You've probably figured out which lines of code we've used to make the white rectangle appear on top of everything.

How it works...

The hint() function can be used to set some hacks for the current renderer. It's mostly used to enable or disable features that are only available for certain renderers. I've used the ENABLE_DEPTH_TEST parameter at the beginning of the draw() function, so that the z buffer is enabled when we draw the grid of cubes and the black square. The DISABLE_DEPTH_TEST parameter is used to disable the z buffer, so that we can draw the white square on top of the other objects.

Drawing triangle and quad strips

Triangle strips are a series of connected triangles. They share vertices and are used for faster rendering. Quad strips are similar, but they are a series of connected quads. Triangle and quad strips are handy if you want to draw circle segments or ribbons in a 3D environment.

How to do it...

Start by importing the OpenGL library, and set up a window of 640 x 480 pixels. The first thing we're going to do is write some code to draw a triangle strip. Type this piece of code inside the draw() function. You'll notice that I've used an extra parameter for the beginShape() function and that I'm adding two vertices with each iteration of the for loop.

```
background( 255 );
lights();

pushMatrix();
translate( width/2, height/2, 0 );
rotateY( radians( frameCount ) );

pushMatrix();
rotateZ( radians( frameCount ) );

fill( 255, 0, 0 );

beginShape( TRIANGLE_STRIP );
for ( int i = 0; i < 20; i++ ) {
  float x1 = cos( radians( i * 10 ) ) * 100;
  float y1 = sin( radians( i * 10 ) ) * 100;
  float x2 = cos( radians( i * 10 + 5 ) ) * ( 180 - i * 4 );
  float y2 = sin( radians( i * 10 + 5 ) ) * ( 180 - i * 4 );

  vertex( x1, y1, 0 );
  vertex( x2, y2, 50 + i );
}
endShape();
popMatrix();
```

The next piece of code is used to draw the quad strip to the screen. The code is almost the same, the only changes being the use of the QUAD_STRIP parameter for beginShape() and the x, y, and z coordinates of the vertices.

```
pushMatrix();
translate( 0, 0, -100 );
rotateZ( radians( -frameCount ) );

fill( 255, 255, 0 );

beginShape( QUAD_STRIP );
for ( int i = 0; i < 20; i++ ) {
  float x1 = cos( radians( i * 10 ) ) * ( 100 + i * 5 );
  float y1 = sin( radians( i * 10 ) ) * ( 100 + i * 5 );
  float x2 = cos( radians( i * 10 + 5 ) ) * 180;
  float y2 = sin( radians( i * 10 + 5 ) ) * 180;

  vertex( x1, y1, 0 );
  vertex( x2, y2, 80 + i * 2 );
}
endShape();
popMatrix();

popMatrix();
```

If you run the example, you'll see the two strips rotate around the center of the screen. The yellow strip is made from quads, the red one from triangles.

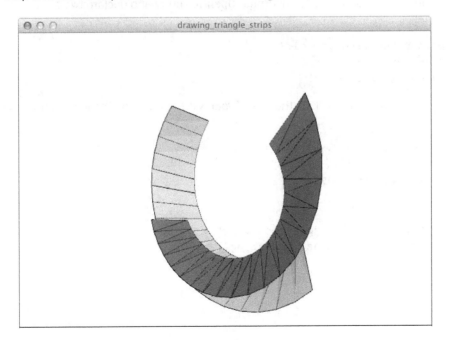

How it works...

You've used the `beginShape()` function in the previous chapter to draw custom shapes. If you don't use a parameter for this function, the vertices are connected with lines in the order you add them, in the `beginShape()` function. If you use TRIANGLE_STRIP or QUAD_STRIP as a parameter, they will be connected with triangles or quads. If you construct these shapes with a `for` loop, you'll usually add two vertices in each iteration.

Using textures

Until now, we've only used plain colors for our 3D objects. But, you can also use images to fill your 3D shape. These images are called textures and can be used to add more character to your 3D scene.

Getting ready

Create two images of 640 x 640 pixels each, and add them to the data folder of your sketch. If you have forgotten how to do this, you can take a look at the recipe *Working with images*, in *Chapter 2, Drawing Text, Curves, and Shapes in 2D*.

How to do it...

The first thing you need to do is to import the OpenGL library and declare two `PImage` objects for your images.

```
import processing.opengl.*;
PImage texture1;
PImage texture2;
```

In the `setup()` function, you'll set the size of your window and load the images from the hard drive.

```
void setup()
{
  size( 640, 480, OPENGL );
  noStroke();

  texture1 = loadImage("stones.jpg");
  texture2 = loadImage("lines.jpg");
}
```

Inside the `draw()` function, we'll draw two squares. We'll add textures to them, using the `texture()` function. For each of these squares, we will map the texture to the vertices in a different way. The first one will be drawn with the `IMAGE` texture mode. The following is the code to draw the square:

```
background( 255 );

textureMode( IMAGE );
pushMatrix();
translate( width/4, height/2, 0 );
rotateY( radians( frameCount ) );
beginShape();
texture( texture1 );
vertex( -100, -100, 0, 0 );
vertex(  100, -100, 640, 0 );
vertex(  100,  100, 640, 640 );
vertex( -100,  100, 0, 640 );
endShape( CLOSE );
popMatrix();
```

For the second square, we'll use the `NORMALIZED` texture mode. The texture image will be mapped, in another way, to the vertices of our shape. You'll notice that the third and fourth parameters of the `vertex()` functions are different.

```
textureMode( NORMALIZED );
pushMatrix();
translate( width*.75, height/2, 0 );
rotateY( radians( -frameCount ) );
beginShape();
texture( texture2 );
vertex( -100, -100, 0, 0 );
vertex(  100, -100, 1, 0 );
vertex(  100,  100, 1, 1 );
vertex( -100,  100, 0, 1 );
endShape( CLOSE );
popMatrix();
```

When you have finished, you can run the example; it should look similar to the following screenshot, depending on the photos you've used.

How it works...

We've learned a few new functions to map the texture images to our shape. Let's take a look at how they work.

▶ The texture() function is used to tell Processing which image should be used as the texture to fill the shape.

▶ The textureMode() function is used to define how Processing should handle the texture to fill your 3D object. The value of the parameter can be either IMAGE or NORMALIZED. The default setting is IMAGE and uses the size of the image as coordinates for the texture mapping. If you use the NORMALIZED texture mode, the texture coordinates will have values between 0 and 1.

▶ The vertex() function has two extra parameters in this example. The first two are the coordinates of your point; the last two are the coordinates for texture mapping. In the IMAGE texture mode, the line vertex(100, -100, 640, 0) will draw a vertex at (100, -100) and map the texture at the image coordinate (640, 0), to that point, which is the upper-right corner of the image. In the NORMALIZED texture mode, the value (1, 0) would refer to the upper right corner of the image.

Using the 3D camera

When you work in 3D, you can move and rotate objects in space, but you can also do this with the camera. In this example, we'll draw a simple scene and animate the camera with the `camera()` function.

How to do it...

You can start by setting up an OpenGL window of 640 x 480 pixels. You also need to declare two float variables named x and z and assign them a value inside the `setup()` function. These variables will be used to animate the camera.

```
import processing.opengl.*;

float x;
float z;

void setup()
{
  size( 640, 480, OPENGL );

  x = 0;
  z = 0;

  noStroke();
}
```

The next thing we'll do is to draw a simple 3D scene. We'll draw a floor with a cube placed in the center of it. I've used the `fill()` function before each vertex to give each corner of the floor a different color. This is probably the easiest way to draw gradients with Processing.

```
background( 255 );
lights();

beginShape();
fill( 255, 0, 0 );
vertex( 0, height, 0);
fill( 255, 255, 0 );
vertex( 0, height, -1000 );
fill( 0, 255, 0 );
vertex( width, height, -1000 );
fill( 0, 0, 255 );
vertex( width, height, 0 );
endShape(CLOSE);
```

```
fill( 255 );
pushMatrix();
translate( width/2, height-50, -500 );
box( 100 );
popMatrix();
```

If you run the sketch, you'll see the scene through the default camera. The next thing we'll do is to animate the camera so it circles around the object, and zooms in and out. Type the following code right after the `lights()` function.

```
x = cos( radians( frameCount ) ) * 1000;
z = sin( radians( frameCount ) ) * 1000;
camera( x, 0, z, width/2, height-50, -500, 0, 1, 0 );
```

If you run the sketch now, you'll see the the scene through the camera we've defined with the `camera()` function. Don't be confused by the animation. The camera is animated, and has a different position in every frame. The scene doesn't move.

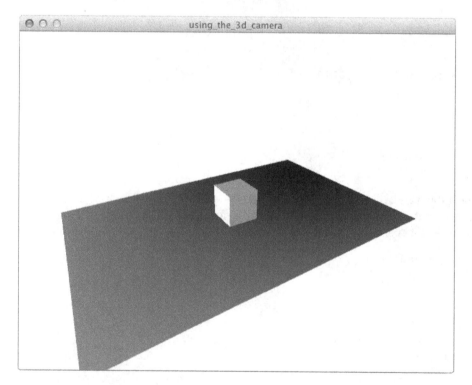

How it works...

The camera() function takes zero or nine parameters. Use the camera() function without parameters to use the default Processing camera. If you want to place the camera at another point in your 3D environment, you'll need to use all nine parameters. The first three parameters are the x, y, and z coordinates for the eye of the camera. The second block of three parameters consists of the x, y, and z coordinates for the center of the scene. The camera in our example is pointed at the cube. The last three parameters take values between -1.0 and 1.0, but you'll usually use -1.0, 0.0, or 1.0. I've used (0, 1, 0) for this, which will be the most common use. If you changed this to (0, -1, 0), the camera would be rotated 180 degrees over the Y-axis, and the scene would be shown upside down. You can experiment by changing these values to get a different result.

There's more...

The camera() function is really hard to use and debug. If you really want control over your scene, you might use the PeasyCam library by Jonathan Feinberg. This library can be downloaded at http://mrfeinberg.com/peasycam/. Another option is the Obsessive Camera Direction (OCD) library by Kristian Linn Damkjer, available for download at http://gdsstudios.com/processing/libraries/ocd/.

4
Working with Data

In this chapter we will cover:

- ▸ Loading text files from the hard drive
- ▸ Parsing CSV
- ▸ Parsing XML
- ▸ Converting datatypes
- ▸ Working with Strings
- ▸ Working with arrays
- ▸ Working with ArrayLists
- ▸ Working with HashMaps

Introduction

In this chapter, we'll mostly print things to the console. There will be little visual output. You'll learn how to load XML and CSV and parse them, so that you can use the data stored in those files. We'll also take a look at some useful data structures, such as ArrayList and HashMap. This chapter will be very handy if you want to get started with data visualization.

Loading text files from the hard drive

This recipe will cover the basics of loading text files from the hard drive. You will also use this technique in some of the other recipes in this chapter.

Getting ready

You'll need a text file with a few lines of text. I've used the poem *My life as a progress meter* by *fridge*. You can read it on the open source poetry website, at `http://opensourcepoetry.org/index.html?poemDisplay.php?poem_id=765`. You need to add the text file to the data folder of your Processing sketch.

How to do it...

We'll start by declaring an array of the type `String`. The `loadStrings()` function inside the `setup()` function will load the text file from the hard drive into the `String` array.

```
String[] textLines;

void setup()
{
  size( 640, 200 );
  smooth();

  textLines = loadStrings("poem.txt");

  noLoop();
}
```

In the `draw()` function, we'll loop through the array and use the number of characters in each line of text to calculate the diameter for the ellipse we'll draw. Each line of text will also be printed to the console.

```
void draw()
{
  background( 255 );
  translate( 20, height/2 );

  stroke( 128 );
  fill( 255, 128 );

  for ( int i = 0; i < textLines.length; i++ ) {
    float d = textLines[i].length();
    ellipse( i * 30, 0, d, d );
    println( i + ". " + textLines[i] );
  }
}
```

If you run the sketch, you'll get the following basic visualization of the poem.

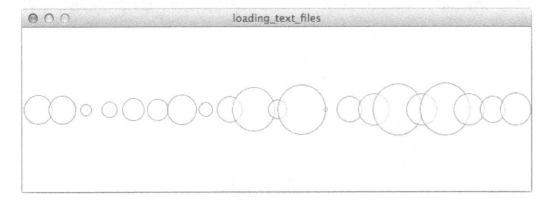

If you take a look at the console of the PDE, you'll see that the lines are printed there, each with their own line number.

```
15. I can sense those who use becoming frustrated, clicking madly
16. their eagerness in clicking is wasted
17. I do not communicate their displeasure to those who toil below
18. they wait in line and do not complain
19. and finally complete their task
20. at 100% my job is done, and I disappear

1
```

How it works...

The `loadStrings()` function is used to load the text file from the hard drive. It returns an array of Strings. Each line of text can be accessed individually. If you want to print the first line of text to the console, you can use `println( textLines[0] )`. If you want to know how many items are there in the array, you can use `textLines.length`. The index of the last item in the array is *length - 1*. If you want to print the last line to the console, you can use `println( textLines[ textLines.length - 1 ] )`.

Parsing CSV

CSV (**Comma Separated Values**) files are text files, commonly used for storing data. Each line contains a row of data. The different pieces of data in each row are separated by a comma. If you open a CSV file in a spreadsheet application such as Microsoft Excel or OpenOffice, you'll notice that each piece of data will be in its own cell. The file I've used looks like the following, if you open it in a text editor.

```
◄  ►  ◊ 🗋  processing-websites.csv  ⬍
1    1, Processing, http://processing.org/
2    2, Processing JS, http://processingjs.org/
3    3, OpenProcessing, http://www.openprocessing.org
4    4, Processing Ghent, http://www.processingghent.org/
5    5, Processing Paris, http://www.processingparis.org/
6    6, Processing Berlin, http://www.processingberlin.com/
7    7, Processing Cities, http://www.processingcities.org/
8    8, Processing Rennes, http://www.processing-rennes.com/
9    9, Processing Bordeaux, http://www.processingbordeaux.org/
10   10, Toxiclibs, http://toxiclibs.org/
```

How to do it...

The first piece of code should look familiar. We've used the `loadStrings()` function in the first recipe of this chapter, to load a text file. We'll use it to load a CSV file here.

```
String[] textLines;

void setup()
{
   textLines = loadStrings("processing-websites.csv");

   noLoop();
}
```

Inside the `draw()` function, we'll loop through the lines of text. The `split()` function is used to split each line into an array with different pieces of data. We'll use a second `for` loop to print these pieces of data to the console.

```
void draw()
{
   background( 255 );
   translate( 20, height/2 );

   stroke( 128 );
```

```
fill( 255, 128 );

for ( int i = 0; i < textLines.length; i++ ) {
  String[] currentLine = split( textLines[i], ", " );
  for ( int j = 1; j < currentLine.length; j++ ) {
    println( currentLine[j] );
  }
  println("---");
}
}
```

The output of the application should look like the following. I've removed some of the results here, to save some space.

```
Processing
http://processing.org/
---
Processing JS
http://processingjs.org/
---
OpenProcessing
http://www.openprocessing.org
---
Processing Ghent
http://www.processingghent.org/
---
Toxiclibs
http://toxiclibs.org/
---
```

How it works...

The most important function to parse CSV files is the `split()` function. The first parameter of this function takes a String variable containing a line of comma separated values. The second parameter is another String variable and contains the characters you want to use to split the first String. In this case, I'm using , (a comma and a space) as the delimiter. The `split()` function will search for these characters in the first String and split it at these points.

There's more...

I've used the `noLoop()` function inside the `setup()` function. This function will stop Processing from continuously executing the code in the `draw()` function. If you use this function in the `setup()` function, this should be on the last line, right before you close the `setup()` function.

If you want to convert data from one format to another, you can use Mr. Data Converter. This is a useful tool to convert data to CSV, XML, or JSON. This is an open source web application written by Shan Carter and can be found at `http://shancarter.com/data_converter/`.

Parsing XML

XML is used by a variety of applications. It's a really handy file format for structuring data that can easily be read by humans and machines. I've used the same data as in the CSV example but converted it to XML. It looks like the following screenshot:

```
     ◄ │ ► │ ○ □  processing-websites.xml  ⬍ │ (no symbol selected)  ⬍
 1      <?xml version="1.0" encoding="UTF-8"?>
 2  ▼   <websites>
 3          <website id="1" url="http://processing.org/">Processing</website>
 4          <website id="2" url="http://processingjs.org/">Processing JS</website>
 5          <website id="3" url="http://www.openprocessing.org/">OpenProcessing</website>
 6          <website id="4" url="http://www.processingghent.org/">Processing Ghent</website>
 7          <website id="5" url="http://www.processingparis.org/">Processing Paris</website>
 8          <website id="6" url="http://www.processingberlin.com/">Processing Berlin</website>
 9          <website id="7" url="http://www.processingcities.org/">Processing Cities</website>
10          <website id="8" url="http://www.processing-rennes.com/">Processing Rennes</website>
11          <website id="9" url="http://www.processingbordeaux.org/">Processing Bordeaux</website>
12          <website id="10" url="http://toxiclibs.org/">Toxiclibs</website>
13  ∟   </websites>
```

How to do it...

The first thing we need to do is to declare an XML object. The `loadXML()` function will be used to load the XML file into this object.

```
XML xml;

void setup()
{
  xml = loadXML( "processing-websites.xml" );
  noLoop();
}
```

Inside the `draw()` function, we'll loop through the XML document and use the `getName()`, `getInt()`, `getString()`, and `getContent()` functions, to get the data out of the structure.

```
void draw()
{
  XML[] kids = xml.getChildren("website");

  for ( int i = 0; i < kids.length; i++ ) {
    int id = kids[i].getInt("id");
```

```
        String url = kids[i].getString("url");
        String txt = kids[i].getContent();
        println( i + ": " + id + " " + url + " " + txt );
    }
}
```

If you run the sketch, you should see the following output in the console:

```
0: 1 http://processing.org/ Processing
1: 2 http://processingjs.org/ Processing JS
2: 3 http://www.openprocessing.org/ OpenProcessing
3: 4 http://www.processingghent.org/ Processing Ghent
4: 5 http://www.processingparis.org/ Processing Paris
5: 6 http://www.processingberlin.com/ Processing Berlin
6: 7 http://www.processingcities.org/ Processing Cities
7: 8 http://www.processing-rennes.com/ Processing Rennes
8: 9 http://www.processingbordeaux.org/ Processing Bordeaux
9: 10 http://toxiclibs.org/ Toxiclibs
```

How it works...

The `xml.getChildren("website")` method, used on the first line of code inside the `draw()` function returns the child nodes named `website`, as an array of XML objects. We'll use a `for` loop to iterate through these objects.

Each `website` node from our XML file has two attributes: `id` and `url`. `id` is an integer and can be accessed with the `xml.getInt()` method. The parameter you need to use for this function is a String with the name of the XML attribute. The `xml.getString()` method is similar to the `xml.getInt()` method and is used to receive the contents from the `url` attribute, as a String.

The `xml.getContent()` method is used to retrieve the data between the opening tag (`<website>`) and closing tag (`</website>`) of the XML node. This method returns a String.

Converting datatypes

While programming, you might run into a situation where you want to convert a variable of the integer type to a float, or a float to a String. In this recipe, we'll take a look at some handy functions you can use to do this.

How to do it...

The code for this example is fairly simple. The functions to convert the data are used within the `println()` function, so that we can directly print the value they return to the console. The following is the full code for the example:

```
int number1 = 65;
float number2 = 7.537;

void setup()
{
  noLoop();
}

void draw()
{
  // convert int to float
  println( float( number1 ) );

  // convert float to int
  println( int( number2 ) );

  // convert a number to a binary string
  println( binary( number1 ) );

  // convert a binary string to a number
  println( unbinary( "0010110011100110" ) );

  // convert numbers or a string to a boolean
  println( boolean( 1 ) );
  println( boolean( number1 ) );
  println( boolean( 0 ) );
  println( boolean("true") );

  // convert char to byte
  println( byte( 'A' ) );

  // convert byte to char
  println( char( number1 ) );

  // convert number and color to hex string
  println( hex( number1 ) );
  println( hex( color( 255, 0, 255 ) ) );
```

```
    // convert hex string to number
    println( unhex( "FF00CC" ) );

    // convert number to string
    println( str( -number2 ) );
}
```

If you run the example, the following lines will be printed to the console:

```
65.0
7
00000000000000000000000001000001
11494
true
true
false
true
65
A
00000041
FFFF00FF
16711884
-7.537
```

How it works...

All functions to convert data types take one parameter. The `binary()` and `hex()` functions can also be used with two parameters.

- The `float()` function is usually used to convert an integer into a float. In our example, the integer 65 is converted to 65.0. You can also use it to convert a String to a float.

- The `int()` function is usually used to convert a float to its integer representation. In our example, the number 7.537 is converted to 7. You can also use it to convert a String to an integer.

- The `binary()` function is used to convert an int, char, or byte to a binary String. If you use the second parameter, you can specify how many digits the function should return. In the example, the number 65 is converted to 00000000000000000000000001000001.

- The `unbinary()` function is the opposite of the `binary()` function. You'll use this one to convert a binary String into an integer.

- ▶ The `boolean()` function is used to convert an integer or String to a boolean variable. If the value of the parameter is `0`, the function will return `false`. Any number that is higher than 0 will return `true`. If you use a String for the parameter, you can use `true` and `false`. Note that you need to add the quotes around these words.

- ▶ The `char()` function is used to convert an integer to a char. In our example, the number `65` is converted to the letter `A`.

- ▶ The `byte()` function is usually used to convert a char or an integer to a byte. The function returns an integer with a value between -128 and 127.

- ▶ The `hex()` function can be used to convert an int, char, byte, or a color into a String with eight hexadecimal digits. If you use the second parameter, you can specify how many digits you want the function to return.

- ▶ The `unhex()` function is the opposite of the `hex()` function. You can use it to convert a String of hexadecimal digits to an integer.

- ▶ The `str()` function is the last one we'll cover and is used to convert any of the other types to a String. In the example, I've used a negative float. The - sign will be added to the String, in this case.

Working with Strings

When you are working with text, you might need to count the characters of a word or change all characters to uppercase. In this recipe, we are going to cover some functions that will come in use when working with text.

How to do it...

The first thing we'll do is declare some String variables and assign some values to them. Strings are basically a sequence of characters, placed between double quotes.

```
String word = "Hello";
String[] textArray;
String wordList = "String,theory,is,confusing";

void setup()
{
  textArray = new String[3];
  textArray[0] = "Man";
  textArray[1] = "Bear";
  textArray[2] = "Pig";

  noLoop();
}
```

Inside the `draw()` function, we'll take a look at the methods we can use on our String variables.

```
println("Word: charAt(1): " + word.charAt(1) );
println("Word: length(): " + word.length() );
println("Word: substring( 2, 4 ): " + word.substring(2, 4) );
println("Word: toLowerCase(): " + word.toLowerCase() );
println("Word: toUpperCase(): " + word.toUpperCase() );
println("Word: indexOf(\"l\"): " + word.indexOf("l") );

if ( word.equals("Hi") ) {
  println("Hi there!");
} else {
  println("The word is not Hi");
}

println("---");
```

Processing also has some functions to work with Strings. You can use these to join an array of String variables into one String, or split a sentence into an array of words.

```
String joined = join( textArray, "" );
println( joined );

println("---");

String[] words = split( wordList, "," );
println( words );

println("---");
println( trim("    I was a sentence with too much whitespace.       ")
);
```

If you run the sketch, the following text will be logged to the console:

```
Word: charAt(1): e
Word: length(): 5
Word: substring( 2, 4 ): ll
Word: toLowerCase(): hello
Word: toUpperCase(): HELLO
Word: indexOf("l"): 2
The word is not Hi
---
ManBearPig
---
[0] "String"
[1] "theory"
```

```
[2] "is"
[3] "confusing"
---
I was a sentence with too much whitespace.
```

How it works...

First, we're going to take a look at how the methods for working with Strings work.

▸ The charAt() method is used to get the character at a certain index. If you want to get the first character, you have to use charAt(0).

▸ The length() method returns the number of characters in the String, as an integer.

▸ The substring() method is used to get a certain part of a String. You can use this method with one or two parameters. If you use it with one parameter, it will return a String starting from the index and continuing to the end of the String. If you use it with two parameters, you can specify the begin index and end index of the part you want to retrieve. In our example, this function returns the characters **ll** of the String Hello, which are at index numbers 2 and 3 in the String. The end index will not be part of the returned String.

▸ The toLowerCase() method converts all characters in the String to lowercase characters. The toUpperCase() method does the opposite and converts all characters to uppercase.

▸ The indexOf() method returns the first appearance of a substring within a String. In our example, it returns the number **2**, which is the index of the first l character found in the String Hello. If the character you search for in the String is hot found, this method will return **-1**.

▸ The equals() function is used to compare a String to another String. It returns true if the Strings are the same and false if they aren't.

There are also some functions available for working with Strings in Processing.

▸ The join() function is used to combine an array of Strings into a single String. I've stitched the words together into one word, but you can use any character or String as the second parameter.

▸ The split() function does the opposite of what the join() function does and splits a String into an array of Strings. We've also used this function in the example on parsing CSV files.

▸ The trim() function is used to remove excessive whitespace from the beginning or end of a String.

Working with arrays

If you only need two variables in your sketch, it's ok to declare them as two different float or int variables. But, if you need lots of variables, this might not be the best option. In this case, you'll need to use an array. An array is basically a collection of variables of the same type. In this recipe, we'll cover how you can work with the functions Processing offers for working with arrays.

How to do it...

The first thing we'll do is to declare two arrays of floats and assign some values to them. You can easily do this by adding curly braces around a series of comma separated numbers.

```
float[] array1 = { 1.0, 4.7, 3.08 };
float[] array2 = { 72.86, 48.32 };

void setup()
{
  noLoop();
}
```

Inside the draw() function, we'll print the output of the functions to the console. The first thing we'll do is add an extra number to the first array by using the append() function.

```
println( "New Array: Array 1 + new float" );
println( "-----------------------------");
float[] newArray = append( array1, 127.75 );
println( newArray );
println();
```

The next thing we'll do is to copy the second array and paste it into the new array we've created by using the arrayCopy() function.

```
println( "Copied Array 2 to New Array" );
println( "-----------------------------");
arrayCopy( array2, 0, newArray, 2, 2 );
println( newArray );
println();
```

If you don't want to copy and paste one array into another one, you can also combine two arrays into a new array using the concat() function.

```
println( "Add array2 to end of array1" );
println( "-----------------------------");
float[] superArray = concat( array1, array2 );
println( superArray );
println();
```

Another function that might come in handy is increasing the size of an array. We're going to take `superArray`, which we've created by combining the first and second array, and use the `expand()` function to do this.

```
println( "Increase the size of an array" );
println( "----------------------------");
println( "Length before expanding: " + superArray.length );
superArray = expand( superArray );
// double length of array
println( "Length after expanding: " + superArray.length);
// expand array to length of 256
superArray = expand( superArray, 256 );
println( "Length after expanding: " + superArray.length );
println();
```

If you want to extract some elements from an array, you can use the `subset()` function. You've done something similar in the *Working with Strings* recipe, when you used the `substring()` method.

```
println( "Extract elements from an array" );
println( "----------------------------");
float[] shortArray = subset( superArray, 1, 4 );
println( shortArray );
```

Of the last two functions we'll use, one is to reverse an array and another is to sort the numbers from small to big.

```
println( "Reverse the order of the array" );
println( "----------------------------");
float[] reversed = reverse( shortArray );
println( reversed );

println( "Sort the values of the array" );
println( "----------------------------");
float[] sorted = sort( shortArray );
println( sorted );
```

When you look at the output of the sketch in the console, you'll see exactly what all these functions do.

```
New Array: Array 1 + new float
----------------------------
[0] 1.0
[1] 4.7
[2] 3.08
[3] 127.75
Copied Array 2 to New Array
```

```
-----------------------------
[0] 1.0
[1] 4.7
[2] 72.86
[3] 48.32
Add array2 to end of array1
-----------------------------
[0] 1.0
[1] 4.7
[2] 3.08
[3] 72.86
[4] 48.32
Increase the size of an array
-----------------------------
Length before expanding: 5
Length after expanding: 10
Length after expanding: 256
Extract elements from an array
-----------------------------
[0] 4.7
[1] 3.08
[2] 72.86
[3] 48.32
Reverse the order of the array
-----------------------------
[0] 48.32
[1] 72.86
[2] 3.08
[3] 4.7
Sort the values of the array
-----------------------------
[0] 3.08
[1] 4.7
[2] 48.32
[3] 72.86
```

How it works...

We've learned some of the basic functions to work with arrays. Let's take a deeper look at what they do.

► The append() function is used to add a single element to the end of the array. The first parameter is the array you want to add a value to, and the second one is the value you want to add. Note that the value should be of the same type as the other elements in the array.

- ▶ The `arrayCopy()` function is used to copy an array, or a part of an array, into another array. In the example, I've used the function with five parameters. The first parameter is used for the source array, and the second one is for the starting point in that array. The third parameter takes the destination array, and the fourth one sets the position in that array. The last parameter specifies the number of elements that should be copied.

- ▶ If you have two arrays of the same type, you can use the `concat()` function to stitch them together into a new array.

- ▶ The `expand()` function is used to increase the size of the array. If you use this function with only one parameter, the size of the array will be doubled. You can add a second parameter to specify the length of the array, if you don't want the size to be doubled.

- ▶ The `subset()` function is used to retrieve a part of the array. The first parameter is used for the array you want to extract from, the second one specifies the position where you want to begin, and the third parameter sets the number of values you want to get.

- ▶ The `reverse()` function is used to reverse the order of the elements in the array.

- ▶ The `sort()` function sorts the values of an array. If you have an array with numbers, just as in our example, they will be sorted from smallest to largest. If you have an array with String variables, they will be sorted alphabetically.

Working with ArrayLists

In the *Working with arrays* recipe, you've learned how to deal with arrays, but working with an array has its limitations. You can't easily add or remove objects. The ArrayList data structure works in a way similar to a regular array of objects, but here you can add or remove objects in a very easy way.

How to do it...

You can start by saving your sketch as `working_with_arraylists.pde`. The next thing you need to do is to add a new tab to your sketch and save it as `MyObject`. You can do this by clicking the arrow icon on top of the PDE or by using the shortcut *Shift + Cmd + N* on the Mac, or *Shift + Ctrl + N* on Windows or Linux.

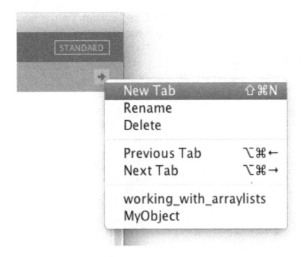

In this tab, we'll write a simple class with two methods. We'll use this class to create objects to fill our ArrayList.

```
class MyObject
{
  float x;
  float y;

  MyObject()
  {
    x = random( width );
    y = random( height );
  }

  void update()
  {
    y--;
  }

  void render()
  {
    ellipse( x, y, 60, 60 );
  }
}
```

Once you've written the code for the `MyObject` class, you can switch back to the `working_with_arraylists` tab to write the `setup()` function.

```
ArrayList<MyObject> myList;

void setup()
{
  size( 640, 480 );
  smooth();

  myList = new ArrayList<MyObject>();
  for ( int i = 0; i < 4; i++ ) {
    myList.add( new MyObject() );
  }
}
```

Inside the `draw()` function, we'll loop backwards through the list of objects, update them, and draw them to the screen. We need to loop backwards through the list, because we are removing elements dynamically.

```
void draw()
{
  background( 255 );

  fill( 255, 128 );
  stroke( 0 );

  for ( int i = myList.size() - 1; i >= 0; i-- ) {
    MyObject o = (MyObject)myList.get( i );
    o.update();
    o.render();
    if ( o.y <= 0 ) {
      myList.remove( i );
    }
  }
}
```

The last part you need to do is to add the `mousePressed()` function. A new object will be added to the list, and the number of elements will be printed to the console if you click the mouse.

```
void mousePressed()
{
  myList.add( new MyObject() );
  println( "Total elements in List: " + myList.size() );
}
```

If you run the sketch, the output will look like the following screenshot:

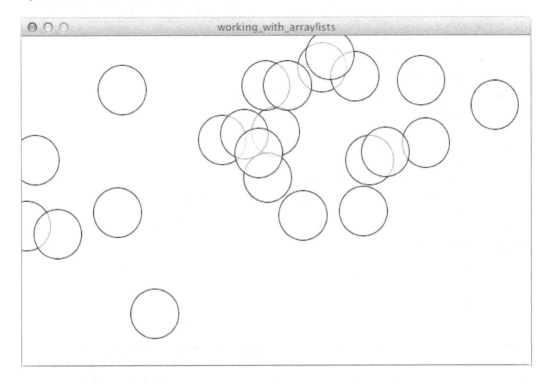

How it works...

The first thing you need to do is declare an `ArrayList` before the `setup()` function. You can simply do this with the following piece of code:

```
ArrayList myList;
```

You can also add a datatype to the list, if you know what objects you'll store in it. I've added the `MyObject` datatype in the example.

```
ArrayList<MyObject> myList;
```

Inside the `setup()` function, you need to create an empty ArrayList. The following lines of code show you how to do it with and without a datatype.

```
myList = new ArrayList(); // without datatype
myList = new ArrayList<MyObject>(); // with datatype
```

You can add objects to the list with the `add()` method. In the example, I've used a regular `for` loop to add four objects. If you want to add a single object, you can do it with the following code:

```
myList.add( new MyObject() );
```

If you want to remove an object from the list, you need to use the `remove()` method. You need to pass the index of the element you want to remove from the list, with this method. If you want to remove the first element, you would call `myList.remove( 0 )`.

There's more...

There are some other ways to loop through an ArrayList. If you add a datatype to your ArrayList, just as you did in the `setup()` function, (`myList = new ArrayList<MyObject>();`), you can use this simplified notation of the `for` loop. You don't need to cast the element you get, to the datatype that you need, any more. This technique also works if you want to loop through an array of objects.

```
for ( MyObject o : myList ) {
    o.update();
    o.render();
}
```

Another way to loop through the ArrayList is to use an Iterator. You can access this Iterator by calling the `iterator()` method on your ArrayList. The `hasNext()` method of the Iterator returns `true`, if there are elements left, and `false`, if you are at the last element. The `next()` method of the Iterator is used to retrieve the next object in the list.

```
Iterator itr = myList.iterator();
while ( itr.hasNext() ) {
    MyObject o = (MyObject)itr.next();
    o.update();
    o.render();
}
```

Working with HashMaps

HashMaps are similar to arrays, but they use a different method for accessing elements. Arrays use an integer for the index, while HashMaps use a String. HashMaps are really useful when you need to search for a specific item in a large collection of data.

How to do it...

We start by declaring a `HashMap` object and adding some values to it, inside the `setup()` function.

```
HashMap<String, Float> hm;

void setup()
{
  hm = new HashMap<String, Float>();
  hm.put("Processing", 51.30);
  hm.put("openFrameworks", 30.45);
  hm.put("Cinder", 12.78);

  noLoop();
}
```

The first thing we'll do inside the `draw()` function is loop through the `HashMap` object using an Iterator and print each entry to the console.

```
Iterator i = hm.entrySet().iterator();
while ( i.hasNext () ) {
  Map.Entry me = (Map.Entry)i.next();
  println( "Key: " + me.getKey() + ", Value: " + me.getValue() );
}
println("---");
```

If you want to check whether a HashMap is empty, you can do that with the `isEmpty()` method. Accessing a single element from the HashMap can be done with the `get()` method.

```
println( "Is Empty? " + hm.isEmpty() );
println( "Get 'Processing': " + hm.get("Processing") );
```

If you want to check how many elements a HashMap contains, you can use the `size()` method. This works the same as with ArrayLists. Removing elements from the HashMap can be done with the `remove()` method.

```
println( "Number of Elements (before remove): " + hm.size() );
println( "Removed: " + hm.remove("openFrameworks") );
println( "Number of Elements (after remove): " + hm.size() );
```

The last thing we'll do is search through the HashMap for whether it contains an entry with a certain key using the `containsKey()` method.

```
println( "Contains key 'openFrameworks': " + hm.containsKey("openFram
eworks") );
```

If you run the example, the following values will be logged to the console:

```
Key: Cinder, Value: 12.78
Key: Processing, Value: 51.3
Key: openFrameworks, Value: 30.45
---
Is Empty? false
Get 'Processing': 51.3
Number of Elements (before remove): 3
Removed: 30.45
Number of Elements (after remove): 2
Contains key 'openFrameworks': false
```

How it works...

You need to declare a HashMap object, first, and initialize it by calling the constructor of the class. It's also a good practice to add the data types you'll store in it. Note that you can only store objects and Strings in a HashMap. This doesn't work for variables of the float or int type. If you do want to store integers or floats in a HashMap, you can use the Integer and Float classes from Java. The Integer class wraps an int variable into an object; the Float class does the same with a float variable.

```
Hashmap<String, Float> hm;
hm = new HashMap<String, Float>();
```

Adding elements can be done with the put() method. The first parameter is the key, and should preferably be a String, so you can easily search for it. The second parameter can be any kind of object. We've used objects of the Float type in our example. To remove objects, you need to use the remove() method. The parameter you need to use for this method is the key from the entry you want to remove.

If you want to check whether a HashMap is empty, you can use the isEmpty() method. This method returns true if the HashMap is empty and false if it contains entries. If you want to check whether a HashMap contains an entry with a certain key, you can use the containsKey() method. The parameter for this function is the key you want to search for. This method also returns a boolean variable.

Looping through all objects in a HashMap can be done with an Iterator. This is similar to working with ArrayLists. The Iterator can be accessed with hm.entrySet().iterator(). Individual entries within a while loop can be accessed with Map.Entry me = (Map. Entry) itr.next(). If you want to get the key or the value for a specific entry, you can use the getKey() and getValue() methods.

5
Exporting from Processing

In this chapter we will cover:

- ▸ Saving images
- ▸ Exporting applications
- ▸ Saving PDF files
- ▸ Calculating PDF sizes
- ▸ Saving text files
- ▸ Exporting 3D files
- ▸ Saving binary files

Introduction

Until now, we've only drawn things to the screen or logged text to the console. But at some point, you'll want to show your art to the world, so you may need to export your work in an appropriate format. Processing can be used to create images, movies, or interactive applications. In this chapter, we'll explore the different ways you can export your work for print, web, or projection.

Saving images

The easiest way to share your work on the web is to upload images to Flickr or Facebook. You could take screenshots of your sketches and use those, but there are better ways to do this. Using the `saveFrame()` function, you can save the contents of your Processing sketch to your hard drive.

How to do it...

We'll use a basic sketch to show how saving images works. The following code will generate 1000 transparent white circles on a black background.

```
void setup()
{
  size( 640, 480 );
  smooth();
}

void draw()
{
  background( 0 );
  for ( int i = 0; i < 1000; i++ ) {
    fill( random( 255 ), 64 );
    stroke( 255, 128 );
    ellipse( random( width ), random( height ), 40, 40 );
  }

  if ( keyPressed ) {
    saveFrame("images/artwork-####.png");
  }
}
```

The saved image will look somewhat like the following image:

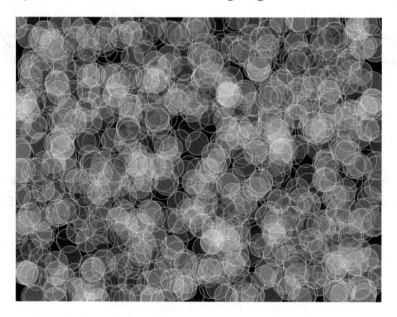

How it works...

Within the draw() function, we'll use the keyPressed system variable. The value of this variable is true if a key is pressed and false if no keys are pressed. The saveFrame() function is used to save the contents of the sketch window to the hard drive. The parameter for this function is a String containing the file name for the image you'll save. I've used images/ at the beginning of this String to tell Processing to save the image in the images directory. You'll find this folder in your sketch folder, after you've run the sketch and saved an image. #### is used to add the current frame number to the image. If you don't use this, existing files will be overwritten. Choosing a file type is very easy. If you use .png at the end of the String, Processing will save a PNG file. If you use .jpg, a JPEG file will be saved. The extensions you can use are .jpg, .png, .tif, and .tga.

If you want to see the images you've saved, you need to check your sketch folder. Go to **Sketch | Show Sketch Folder** to open the images.

Exporting applications

If you need to show one of your interactive sketches in an exhibition, you'll most likely show it on a screen or project it on a wall. But you can't expect the people at the museum to run your sketch from Processing every day before the exhibition opens. A great thing about Processing, is that you can use it to create native fullscreen applications that run on Mac OS X, Windows, or Linux. In the following example, you'll learn how to do this.

How to do it...

You can start by creating a simple animated sketch The size of the sketch will be set dynamically, depending on the screen resolution of the computer you'll run it on. You can do this by using the displayWidth and displayHeight system variables as parameters for the size() function.

```
float x;
float y;
int b;

void setup()
{
  size( displayWidth, displayHeight );
  smooth();

  x = 0;
  y = 0;

  background( 0 );
```

```
    noFill();
  }

  void draw()
  {
    b++;
    if ( b > 255 ) {
      b = 0;
    }

    x += random( 2, 6 );
    if ( x > width ) {
      x = 0;
      y += random( 20, 40 );
      if ( y > height ) {
        y = 0;
      }
    }

    stroke( 0, random( 255 ), b, 64 );
    float r = random( 6, 60 );
    ellipse( x, y, r, r );
  }
```

Once you've finished coding, you can export the application. Go to the **File | Export Application** menu or use the *Cmd + E* shortcut on the Mac, or *Ctrl + E* on Windows or Linux. On the **Export Options** panel, you can choose any of the three platforms and whether you want the application to run fullscreen or not. If you click on the **Export** button, your sketch folder will open and the applications for each of the chosen platforms will be there.

How it works...

Processing will take the code from your sketch and will wrap it in a Java file. You'll find this Java file in the source directory next to the application. The file will be compiled by Processing, using a Java compiler in a native application. This process is done in the background so you don't have to worry about anything.

Saving PDF files

If you want to print your artwork and you save your sketch as an image, the size of your print will be based on the resolution of your image. If you want to print your images really big, you might want to save your sketch as a PDF file. Every shape you draw in Processing is vector-based and can thus be printed at any size. Note that if you work with pixels in Processing, you won't be able to save your work as PDF.

How to do it...

The first thing you need to do is to import the PDF library into your sketch. Go to **Sketch | Import Library | pdf** to do this. You also need to declare a boolean variable named `savePDF`.

```
import processing.pdf.*;

boolean savePDF = false;

void setup()
{
  size( 640, 480 );
  smooth();
  rectMode( CENTER );
  stroke(0);
}
```

Inside the `draw()` function, we'll use the `savePDF` variable to tell Processing when it needs to start recording the PDF file. Everything you draw between the `beginRecord()` and `endRecord()` functions will be included in the PDF file. The `keyPressed()` function is used to change the value of the `savePDF` variable.

```
void draw()
{
  if ( savePDF ) {
    beginRecord( PDF, "pdf/myartwork-####.pdf" );
  }

  background( 0 );
  for ( int i = 0; i < 1000; i++ ) {
    fill( 0, random( 255 ), random( 255 ), 64 );
    pushMatrix();
    translate( random( width ), random( height ) );
    rotate( radians( random( 360 ) ) );
    rect( 0, 0, 50, 50 );
    popMatrix();
  }

  if ( savePDF ) {
    endRecord();
    savePDF = false;
  }
}

void keyPressed()
```

```
  {
    if ( key == 's' ) {
      savePDF = true;
    }
  }
```

If you run the sketch, you can save your work by pressing the S key. You will find the PDF files in the `pdf` folder inside your sketch folder.

How it works...

The `beginRecord()` function is used to tell Processing that it needs to start recording the data that is drawn to the screen. The first parameter for this function is the renderer; in our case this will be `PDF`. The second parameter is a String with the name of the file you want to save. I've used `pdf/myartwork-####.pdf` in the example. The files will be saved in the `pdf` folder; the `####` characters will be replaced with the current frame number. When you are finished drawing, you need to call the `endRecord()` function, so that Processing can save the file to the hard drive.

There's more...

There are different ways to save PDF files from Processing. You can, for instance, save PDF files with multiple pages or flatten your 3D artwork and save it in a PDF file. As I can only cover this basic recipe in my book, you should take a look at the Processing reference to find out how the other techniques work. You can find it at `http://processing.org/reference/libraries/pdf/index.html`.

Calculating PDF sizes

Imagine that you need to generate a few thousand vector images to print postcards. To streamline your process, you probably want to generate PDF files with the exact dimensions, so that you don't have to crop them manually.

How to do it...

You need to define the size of your final print first. Let's say that you'll use a standard A4 sheet of paper. The dimensions of this piece of paper are 210 x 297 millimeters, or 8.2677 x 11.6929 inches. The final size of your sketch will be 595 x 842 pixels. You can define the size of an A4 sheet of paper inside the `setup()` function, as done in the following code:

```
void setup()
{
  size( 595, 842 );
}
```

How it works...

The only thing you need to know is that Processing displays everything on the screen with a resolution of 72 dots per inch (DPI). If you use the metric system, you'll need to convert the size of your final output from millimeters to inches first. One inch is 25.4 millimeters. If you use the imperial system, you won't need to convert anything. The next thing you need to do is to convert from inches to pixels. To do this, you need to multiply the number of inches by 72 and round it to the nearest integer value. A standard letter size page is 8.5 x 11 inches. The calculation to convert these dimensions to pixels is as follows:

8.5 x 72 = 612 pixels

11 x 72 = 792 pixels

Saving text files

In the previous chapter, you learned about opening text files. We'll take a look at how you can save them.

How to do it...

The first thing you'll need to do is declare an object of the `PrintWriter` type and initialize it with the `createWriter()` function.

```
PrintWriter textFile;

void setup()
{
  textFile = createWriter("files/randomnumbers.txt");
}
```

In each cycle of the `draw()` function, we'll write a random number to the file. When the `frameCount` variable reaches 1000, we'll save the file and quit the application.

```
void draw()
{
  textFile.println( random( 200 ) );
  if ( frameCount >= 1000 ) {
    textFile.flush();
    textFile.close();
    exit();
  }
}
```

How it works...

The `createWriter()` function is used to create a text file. The parameter for this file is a String containing the file name. Just like in the example on saving images, I've added a file directory to the String.

Inside the `draw()` function, you'll use the `textFile.println()` method. This method works just like the `println()` function but writes the line of text to the file instead of the console.

Saving the file is done with the `flush()` method, followed by the `close()` method. You have to use both of these methods to ensure that the file is made correctly.

Exporting 3D files

You've already learned that you can save your work as an image or a PDF file. If you want to generate 3D objects in Processing, and render them in a 3D application such as Cinema 4D or in a CAD program, you'll need to save that 3D data. We'll take a look at how you can use the DXF library that comes with Processing to save your generated 3D models.

How to do it...

We'll need to import the DXF and OpenGL libraries first. Go to the **Sketch | Import Library** menu, and choose these libraries from there. You'll also need to declare a boolean variable named `saveDXF`. We'll use this variable in the same way as we used the `savePDF` variable in the recipe on saving PDF files.

```
import processing.opengl.*;
import processing.dxf.*;

boolean saveDXF = false;

void setup()
{
  size( 640, 480, OPENGL );
  smooth();
}
```

In the `draw()` function, we'll use the `beginRaw()` and `endRaw()` functions to record the 3D data we need to save. You need to draw all 3D objects between these functions.

```
void draw()
{
  if ( saveDXF == true ) {
    beginRaw( DXF, "files/myCubes.dxf" );
  }

  lights();

  background( 255 );
  fill( 128 );
  noStroke();

  for ( int i = 0; i < 100; i++ ) {
    pushMatrix();
    translate(random(width), random(height), random(-1000,
0));
    pushMatrix();
    rotateX( radians( random( 360 ) ) );
    rotateY( radians( random( 360 ) ) );
    rotateZ( radians( random( 360 ) ) );
    box( 50 );
    popMatrix();
    popMatrix();
  }

  if ( saveDXF == true ) {
    endRaw();
    saveDXF = false;
  }
}

void keyPressed()
{
  if ( key == 's' ) {
    saveDXF = true;
  }
}
```

How it works...

The `beginRaw()` and `endRaw()` functions are used to capture 3D data and write it to a file. You can use them to write your 3D scene to a PDF file, where it will be flattened. If you want the actual 3D data, you need to save the data to a `.dxf` file. The first parameter of the `beginRecord()` function is either DXF or PDF, the second one is the name of the file you want to save.

If you want to see the contents of your DXF file, you can use the free eDrawings Viewer software, which is available for Windows and Mac OS X. You can download it at `http://www.edrawingsviewer.com/`. If you open the file in this application, it should look somewhat like the following screenshot:

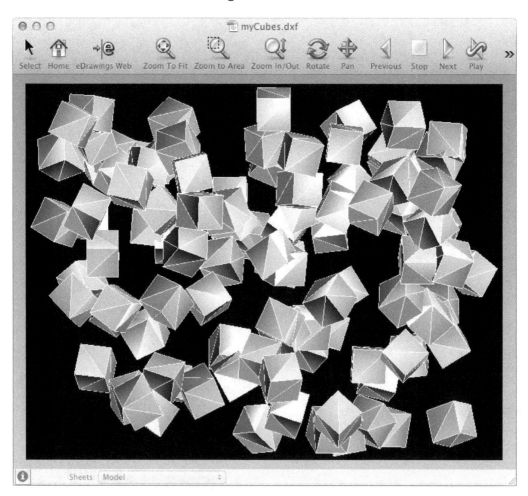

There's more...

You can use Hemesh or Toxiclibs to generate 3D geometry and save everything as STL files. This file format is much more usable for rapid prototyping.

Saving binary files

You've already learned that Processing can save data to a text file. In this recipe, we'll take a look at how you can write data to a binary file. This might be useful when you want to create your own proprietary file format.

How to do it...

You need to declare an integer array with a length of 1000 before the `setup()` function. When you run the sketch, this array will be filled with some random numbers representing uppercase and lowercase letters of the alphabet.

```
int[] numbers = new int[1000];

void setup()
{
  for ( int i = 0; i < numbers.length; i++ ) {
    if ( random( 100 ) < 50 ) {
      // uppercase A - Z
      numbers[i] = floor( random( 65, 91 ) );
    } else {
      // lowercase a - z
      numbers[i] = floor( random( 97, 123 ) );
    }
  }
}
```

Inside the `draw()` function, we'll convert the integer array into a byte array and use the `saveBytes()` method to save the data to the hard drive.

```
void draw()
{
  if ( keyPressed ) {
    byte[] bytes = byte( numbers );
    saveBytes( "strangefile-"+frameCount+".zzz", bytes
);
    exit();
  }
}
```

How it works...

The saveBytes() function is used to save an array of bytes to the hard drive. The first parameter is a String representing the name of the file you want to save, while the second parameter is the array of bytes.

If you open the saved file in a text editor, you'll see lots of strange characters. If you want to see the real data, you'll need to open it in a hex editor. I've used HexEdit on Mac OS X; similar applications are available for Windows or Linux. The following screenshot shows the contents of the file we've just saved. You'll see that the column on the right-hand side contains lowercase and uppercase characters.

There's more...

If you want to open the file you've just saved, you can use the loadBytes() function. The following piece of code will print all characters you see in the right-hand side column of the hex editor screenshot, to the console. That is, it will if you've used the same file as I did.

```
byte[] bytes = loadBytes("strangefile-56.zzz");
println( char( bytes ) );
```

6
Working with Video

In this chapter we will cover:

- ▸ Playing a video
- ▸ Exporting image sequences
- ▸ Manipulating pixels in a video
- ▸ Using filters
- ▸ Controlling the speed of a video
- ▸ Jumping to a specific frame
- ▸ Blending video

Introduction

Until now, we've only drawn shapes and images on the screen. In this chapter, we'll take a look at how you can draw video files, blend them together, or use filters to create a more interesting effect. You'll also learn how you can export your work as an image sequence, so that you can create a video file to show your work on websites such as Vimeo or YouTube.

Playing a video

This will be the most basic recipe in this chapter. You'll learn how to load a video file from the hard drive and play it on the screen.

Getting ready

Start a new Processing sketch, and save it in your sketch folder as `playing_video.pde`. Add a video file to the data folder of the sketch by dragging the video file onto the Processing window. I've used the `marbles.mov` file for all examples; you can use this one too, if you like. This video file should be in the data folder of your Processing sketch. You can add it by dragging the file onto the PDE.

How to do it...

You need to start by importing the `video` library. Go to **Sketch | Import Library | video**, to do this. You also need to declare a `Movie` object, right before the `setup()` function. Inside the `setup()` function, you'll load the video file from the hard drive, and set the video to loop.

```
import processing.video.*;

Movie m;

void setup()
{
  size( 640, 480 );

  m = new Movie( this, "marbles.mov" );
  m.loop();
}
```

The next thing you need to do is write the `movieEvent()` function to read a new frame from the video file.

```
void movieEvent( Movie m )
{
  m.read();
}
```

The last thing you'll do is draw the current video frame to the screen, using the `image()` function.

```
void draw()
{
  background( 0 );
  image( m, 0, 0, width, height );
}
```

The end result will look like the following screenshot, if you've used the same video file.

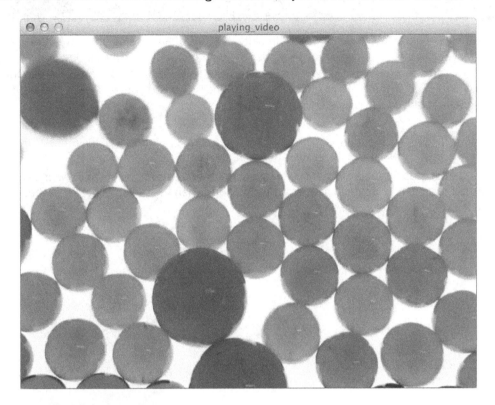

How it works...

The first thing you'll do is to declare an object of the type Movie. You need to do this before the setup() function. Inside the setup() function, we'll load the movie file from the data folder of the sketch into the object, using the new Movie() method. This constructor takes two parameters. The first one will be the this keyword. This will pass a reference from the main PApplet object to the new Movie object. The second parameter is a String with the name of the video file. I've used the loop() method of the Movie class to continuously play the video.

The movieEvent() function is called automatically every time a new frame is available. You need to use the read() method of the Movie class to capture the frame. You can draw this frame to the screen using the image() function.

Exporting image sequences

Processing is a great tool to make videos. In older versions of Processing, there was the MovieMaker class, which allowed you to render the output of your sketch to a QuickTime movie. This class has been removed from Processing 2, as it uses the GStreamer framework now, instead of QuickTime. In this recipe, you'll learn how to export your work as an image sequence, so that you can create a video file afterwards.

How to do it...

This is the full code for the example. I've used an array of PVector objects to draw lines and circles to the screen, animated using Brownian motion. When the running sketch reaches frame 900, the application will quit.

```
int randomNum;
  1
PVector[] points;

float radius = 2;

void setup()
{
  size( 1280, 720 )
  smooth();

  background( 234, 228, 17 );

  points = new PVector[64];
  for ( int i = 0; i < points.length; i++ ) {
    points[i] = new PVector(random(width), random(height));
  }

  frameRate( 30 );

  randomNum = floor( random( 10000, 90000 ) );

  noFill();
  stroke( 0, 64 );
}

void draw()
{
  for ( int i = 0; i < points.length; i++ ) {
    float newX = points[i].x + random( -10, 10 );
```

```
    float newY = points[i].y + random( -10, 10 );

    stroke( i*4, 64 );

    line( points[i].x, points[i].y, newX, newY );
    ellipse( newX, newY, radius, radius );

    points[i].x = newX;
    points[i].y = newY;
  }

  radius++;
  if ( radius > 10 ) {
    radius = 2;
  }

  saveFrame("images/export-"+randomNum+"-#####.tga");

  // save 900 frames = 30 sec @ 30 fps
  if ( frameCount >= 900 ) {
    exit();
  }
}
```

After you run the sketch, you'll find the TGA image sequence in the images folder of your sketch folder.

Name	Date Modified	Size	Kind
export_image_sequences.pde	Today 12:17	1 KB	Processing Sc
images	Today 12:17	--	Folder
export-31771-00001.tga	Today 12:17	35 KB	TGA image
export-31771-00002.tga	Today 12:17	40 KB	TGA image
export-31771-00003.tga	Today 12:17	47 KB	TGA image
export-31771-00004.tga	Today 12:17	55 KB	TGA image
export-31771-00005.tga	Today 12:17	64 KB	TGA image
export-31771-00006.tga	Today 12:17	73 KB	TGA image
export-31771-00007.tga	Today 12:17	84 KB	TGA image
export-31771-00008.tga	Today 12:17	94 KB	TGA image
export-31771-00009.tga	Today 12:17	105 KB	TGA image
export-31771-00010.tga	Today 12:17	107 KB	TGA image
export-31771-00011.tga	Today 12:17	111 KB	TGA image
export-31771-00012.tga	Today 12:17	116 KB	TGA image
export-31771-00013.tga	Today 12:17	122 KB	TGA image
export-31771-00014.tga	Today 12:17	130 KB	TGA image
export-31771-00015.tga	Today 12:17	138 KB	TGA image
export-31771-00016.tga	Today 12:17	147 KB	TGA image

How it works...

The most important thing, when you create movies, is to set the right size and frame rate in the setup() function of your sketch. I've used a size of 1280 x 720 pixels and set the frame rate to 30 frames per second. This will give you a good idea of what the movie will look like when you run the sketch without saving images. This video format is good for sharing your video on video websites, such as Vimeo and YouTube. Note that if you do some heavy calculations each frame, this may slow the sketch down, and the actual frame rate will be less than the one you've set with the frameRate() function.

Each frame of your sketch will be saved, using the saveFrame() function. I've used a random integer named randomNum in the filename of the images, so that you'll be able to save more than one image sequence in the same directory. It might also be a good idea to quit your sketch after saving the image sequence. You can do this by using the exit() function. If you want a video of 30 seconds, you need to save 900 frames. Calculating this number is very easy: *number of frames per second x number of seconds = total number of frames.*

I've saved the images as a TGA sequence. This is the fastest way of saving images with Processing, as the TGA file format is uncompressed. Alternatively, you can use PNG or JPEG, but you'll notice that this will slow down your sketch.

Manipulating pixels in a video

In the first recipe of this chapter, you've learned how to load a video file and display its frames to the screen using the image() function. In this recipe, we'll take a look at how we can change the appearance of the movie by changing the color of some of the pixels.

How to do it...

The first part of the sketch will be similar to the example from the first recipe. Import the video library, declare a Movie object, load the video file, and loop it.

```
import processing.video.*;

Movie m;
int numPixels;

void setup()
{
  size( 640, 480 );

  numPixels = width * height;

  m = new Movie( this, "marbles.mov" );
  m.loop();
}
```

The big changes for this example are in the `draw()` function. We'll draw each frame of the movie to the screen, using the `image()` function. After doing that, we'll change the color of the pixels with a brightness higher than 245.

```
void draw()
{
  background( 0 );
  image( m, 0, 0, width, height );

  loadPixels();
  for ( int i = 0; i < numPixels; i++ ) {
    float b = brightness( pixels[i] );
    if ( b > 245 ) {
      pixels[i] = lerpColor( pixels[i], color(0, 0, 0), map(b, 0, 255,
0, 1));
    }
  }
  updatePixels();
}

void movieEvent( Movie m )
{
  m.read();
}
```

If you run the sketch, you'll see that a lot of the screen will be black because the movie we've used is very bright.

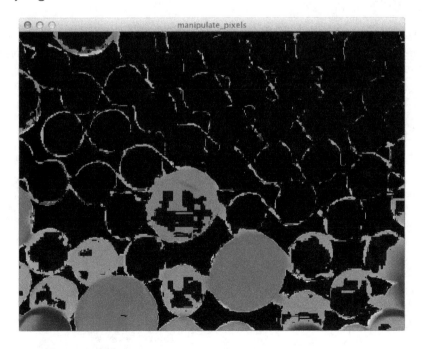

How it works...

After drawing the image to the screen, I've used the `loadPixels()` function to load all pixels from the screen to the pixels array. I've used a `for` loop to go over all pixels, to check their brightness. If the brightness of a pixel is higher than `245`, the pixel color is mixed with black. After changing the colors, you need to call the `updatePixels()` function to show the manipulated image on the screen.

The `lerpColor()` function is used to mix two colors. The first two parameters of this function are used for the colors you want to mix, and the third parameter is used to define how these colors are mixed. This should be a value between 0 and 1. If you use 0.1, the resulting color will be visually very close to the first color. If you use 0.9, it will look more like the second color. If you want to mix both colors equally, you can use 0.5.

If you use a video that isn't as bright as this one, you can lower the brightness threshold value. This will give you a different result. You can also try using the `hue()` or the `saturation()` values of a pixel as a threshold value for coloring the pixels.

Using filters

Filters are probably the easiest way to change the appearance of your video. In this recipe, you'll learn how to use the `filter()` function and the different *presets* you can use with it.

How to do it...

The code for this example is the same as the code you've used in the first recipe from this chapter. The only difference is that you'll use the `filter()` function right after you've drawn the movie to the screen, using the `image()` function.

```
import processing.video.*;

Movie m;

void setup()
{
  size( 640, 480 );

  m = new Movie( this, "marbles.mov" );
  m.loop();
}

void draw()
{
  background( 0 );
```

```
    image( m, 0, 0, width, height );
    filter( POSTERIZE, 4 );
}

void movieEvent( Movie m )
{
    m.read();
}
```

I've used the `filter()` function with the `POSTERIZE` mode, in this example. The result will look like the following screenshot:

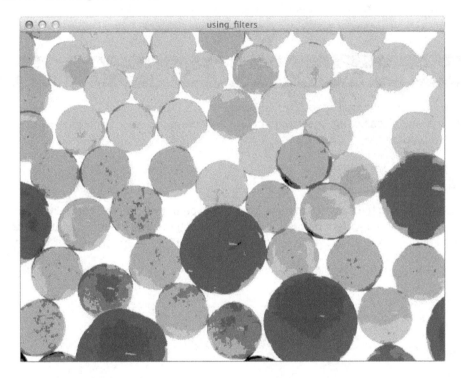

How it works...

The `filter()` function usually takes one parameter to change the appearance of what is shown on the screen. Some modes also need a second parameter. The following are modes you can use with the `filter()` function:

   ▸   BLUR: This mode applies a Gaussian blur filter to the pixels on the screen. The second parameter sets the radius of the blur. If you use this mode without specifying a second parameter, the radius of the blur will be 1 pixel. Note that your sketch will slow down, if you use a big blur radius.

- ▶ `DILATE`: This mode increases the light areas of the image. It is handy if you want less contrast.

- ▶ `ERODE`: This one does the opposite of what the `DILATE` mode does—it decreases the light areas of the image. You can use this one if you want to add more contrast to the image.

- ▶ `GRAY`: This mode converts the video to grayscale.

- ▶ `INVERT`: This mode converts the image to its negative.

- ▶ `OPAQUE`: This mode converts the alpha channel of the image to opaque pixels.

- ▶ `POSTERIZE`: This mode reduces the number of colors in the image. The second parameter sets the number of colors.

- ▶ `THRESHOLD`: This mode converts the image to black and white pixels.

Controlling the speed of a video

Playing a video at its normal speed can be boring. In this recipe, we'll take a look at how you can make a video less boring. You'll learn how to speed up your video, slow it down, and even play it backwards.

How to do it...

We'll start again with the same code as in the first recipe of this chapter, but we'll declare a `float` variable named s, right before the `setup()` function. We'll use this variable to control the speed of the movie, so you need to assign it a value of `1.0` in the `setup()` function.

```
import processing.video.*;

Movie m;
float s;

void setup()
{
  size( 640, 480 );

  m = new Movie( this, "marbles.mov" );
  m.loop();

  s = 1.0;
}
```

Inside the draw function, we'll draw the current frame to the screen, using the `image()` function. We'll draw the value of the `Speed` variable to the screen, using the `text()` function. The `movieEvent()` function stays the same.

```
void draw()
{
  background( 0 );
  image( m, 0, 0, width, height );

  fill( 0 );
  text( "Speed: " + s, 20, 20 );
}

void movieEvent( Movie m )
{
  m.read();
}
```

The mousePressed() function will be used to set the speed of the movie. We'll map the value of the mouseX variable, so it fits within the -2 to 2 range. We'll use the speed() method of the Movie class to set the playback speed of the movie to this value.

```
void mousePressed()
{
  s = map( mouseX, 0, width, -2, 2 );
  m.speed( s );
}
```

Run the sketch and click on the screen, to see the following screenshot:

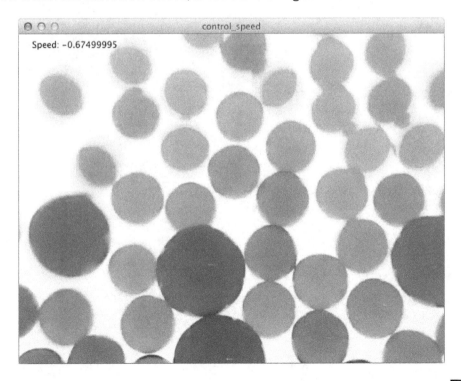

How it works...

The `speed()` method of the `Movie` class is used to set the playback speed of the video. If you use a speed of 1.0, the video will play back at its normal speed. If you use 0.5, the video will play at half its normal speed. If you want to play the video faster, you need to use a number that is higher than 1.0. Negative numbers will play the video backwards.

Jumping to a specific frame

In the previous recipe, you learned how to control the speed of your movie. In this one, we'll take a look at how you can jump to a specific position inside the video file.

How to do it...

We'll start with the same code as in the first recipe, but we'll add a `float` variable named w, which we will use to draw a progress bar to the screen.

```
import processing.video.*;

Movie m;
float w;

void setup()
{
  size( 640, 480 );

  m = new Movie( this, "marbles.mov" );
  m.loop();
}

void draw()
{
  background( 0 );
  image( m, 0, 0, width, height );

  fill( 0 );
  noStroke();
  rect( 0, 0, w, 10 );
}
```

The `movieEvent()` function looks a little different. We'll map the current time of the movie to a value between `0` and the `width` of our sketch window and store it in the `w` variable.

```
void movieEvent( Movie m )
{
  m.read();
  w = map( m.time(), 0, m.duration(), 0, width );
}
```

In the `mousePressed()` function, we'll map the value of the `mouseX` variable to a range between `0` and the duration of the movie and use the `jump()` method to make the playhead jump to that time in the movie.

```
void mousePressed()
{
  float x = map( mouseX, 0, width, 0, m.duration() );
  m.jump( x );
}
```

Run the sketch and click on the window to see what happens. The result will look like the following screenshot:

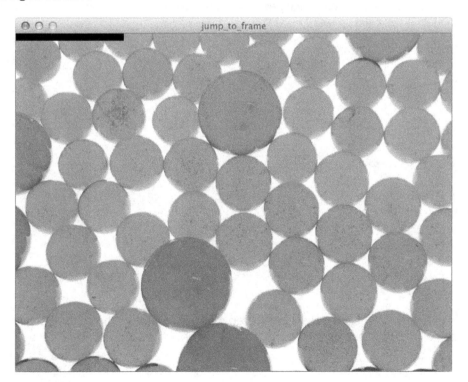

How it works...

The duration() method of the Movie class returns a float value containing the total duration of the movie in seconds. The time() method returns the current position of the playhead in seconds. The jump() method is used to set the playhead to another position in the movie. The parameter for this function is a float value between 0 and the duration of the movie. The black bar you see on top of the screen is the progress bar. The width of this rectangle is calculated in the movieEvent() function.

Blending video

This recipe will be a little different. We'll play two different movies at the same time and blend them together. You'll learn how to use the different blending modes to get some really psychedelic results.

How to do it...

We'll start by declaring two Movie objects, one for each video. I've used the original marbles video and the marbles2 video, which has a kaleidoscope effect applied to it. We'll run this second video at twice the speed.

```
import processing.video.*;

Movie m1;
Movie m2;

void setup()
{
  size( 640, 480 );

  m1 = new Movie( this, "marbles.mov" );
  m1.loop();

  m2 = new Movie( this, "marbles2.mov" );
  m2.loop();
  m2.speed( 2 );
}
```

The movieEvent() function looks a little different. If you have more than one video playing at the same time, you need to read the frames separately.

```
void movieEvent( Movie m )
{
  if ( m == m1 ) {
```

```
    m1.read();
  } else {
    m2.read();
  }
}
```

Inside the `draw()` function, we'll draw the first movie to the screen. The second movie will be drawn on the screen, using the `blend()` function.

```
void draw()
{
  background( 0 );
  image( m1, 0, 0, width, height );

  blend(m2, 0, 0, width, height, 0, 0, width, height, DIFFERENCE);
}
```

The result of this technique will look somewhat like the following image, depending on the blending mode you've used.

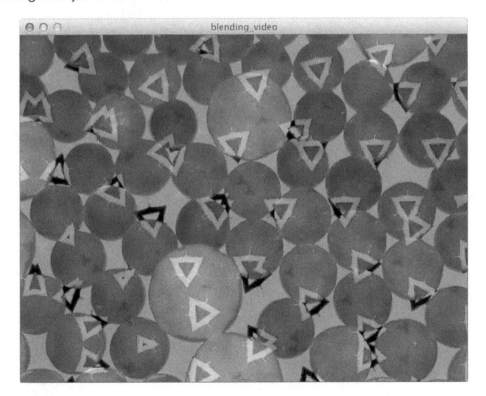

How it works...

The `blend()` function takes a lot of parameters. The first one takes a `PImage` object, in our case the current frame of the movie. The next four parameters take the *x* and *y* coordinates and the width and height of the source image. Parameters six to nine do the same for the destination image. The last parameter is the blending mode. These modes work the same way as the blending modes in image editors, such as Photoshop. These are the available modes: ADD, BLEND, BURN, DARKEST, DIFFERENCE, DODGE, EXCLUSION, HARD_LIGHT, LIGHTEST, MULTIPLY, OVERLAY, SCREEN, SOFT_LIGHT, and SUBTRACT. Go ahead and play around with these modes to see the effect they have on the final output of your sketch.

7
Audio Visualization

In this chapter we will cover:

- ▶ Importing the Minim library
- ▶ Playing audio files
- ▶ Using live audio
- ▶ Drawing a waveform
- ▶ Using Fast Fourier Transforms
- ▶ Audio reactive particles
- ▶ Creating a drum machine
- ▶ Creating a synthesizer
- ▶ Using effects

Introduction

In this chapter, we'll take a look at how you can work with audio. You'll learn how to play audio files and visualize them. You'll also learn how to make simple instruments, such as a drum computer and a synthesizer. We'll finish the chapter with a recipe on working with effects.

Throughout this chapter, we'll use Minim, the audio library that is included with Processing. But there are some other libraries available to work with audio that might be better for the thing you want to do. Here are some of them:

- ▶ Sonia, by *Amit Pitaru*, can be found at `http://sonia.pitaru.com/`
- ▶ Beads, by *Ollie Bown*, can be found at `http://www.beadsproject.net/`
- ▶ Ess, by *Krister Olsson*, can be found at `http://www.tree-axis.com/Ess/`

Importing the Minim library

The first thing you'll need to do for every sketch in this chapter is to import the `minim` library. You'll learn all about Minim in this recipe.

How to do it...

Create a new sketch and go to **Sketch | Import Library | minim**. The following lines will be added at the top of your document.

```
import ddf.minim.*;
import ddf.minim.signals.*;
import ddf.minim.analysis.*;
import ddf.minim.effects.*;
```

How it works...

The `minim` library contains four packages. These contain specific classes to work with a certain aspect of audio. You don't usually need to import all of them into your sketch.

- `ddf.minim.*`: This contains the main `Minim` classes. You'll need to import this one in every sketch where you want to use the `minim` library. This package allows you to play audio files and work with the microphone input of your computer.

- `ddf.minim.signals.*`: This contains an oscillator and some wave generators to create sine waves, saw waves, and so on. This package is mostly used to create synthesizers.

- `ddf.minim.analysis.*`: This contains classes to analyze audio. There's a class to do some simple beat detection and one to do Fast Fourier Transforms.

- `ddf.minim.effects.*`: This contains some classes to add effects to your audio. These effects are basically filters that allow you to filter out some frequencies from an audio stream.

Playing audio files

We'll start with the easiest thing you can do with Minim, and that is playing an audio file. But since this might be a little too easy, we'll add a basic interface, so that you can control the audio with your keyboard and mouse.

Getting ready

Create a new sketch and save it as `playing_audio_files.pde`. Import the `minim` library to your sketch, just like you learned in the first recipe of this chapter. You also need to add an MP3 file to your sketch. Go find your favorite song on your hard drive and drag it onto the Processing editor to add it to the data folder of your sketch.

How to do it...

The first thing we need to do is declare a `Minim` object and an `AudioPlayer` object, right before the `setup()` function.

```
Minim minim;
AudioPlayer player;
```

Inside the `setup()` function, we'll initialize the `minim` object, load the MP3 file from the data folder, and play it.

```
void setup()
{
  size( 640, 480 );

  minim = new Minim( this );

  player = minim.loadFile("song.mp3");
  player.play();
}
```

Inside the `draw()` function, we'll draw some basic information about the song. There will be a line that shows the current position of the playhead and some text with the same information.

```
void draw()
{
  background( 255 );

  float x = map(player.position(), 0, player.length(), 0, width);

  stroke( 0 );
  line( x, 0, x, height );

  int totalSeconds = (int)(player.length()/1000) % 60;
  int totalMinutes = (int)(player.length()/(1000*60)) % 60;
  int playheadSeconds = (int)(player.position()/1000) % 60;
  int playheadMinutes = (int)(player.position()/(1000*60)) % 60;
```

```
String info = "Position: " + playheadMinutes + ":" + nf(
playheadSeconds, 2 ) + "/" + totalMinutes + ":" + nf(
totalSeconds, 2 );

fill( 0 );
noStroke();
text( info, 10, 20 );
}
```

Next up is adding some interaction to the sketch. The code is very straightforward, and you should be able to read it by now.

```
void mousePressed()
{
  int pos = floor( map( mouseX, 0, width, 0, player.length() ) );
  player.play( pos );
}

void keyPressed()
{
  if ( key == ' ' ) {
    if ( player.isPlaying() ) {
      player.pause();
    } else {
      player.play();
    }
  }

  if ( key == CODED ) {
    if ( keyCode == LEFT ) {
      player.rewind();
    }
  }
}
```

You also need to add the `stop()` function to your sketch, so the `AudioPlayer` object can be closed, and the `Minim` object can be stopped when we quit the sketch. Don't forget this.

```
void stop()
{
  player.close();
  minim.stop();
  super.stop();
}
```

If you run the sketch, the result will look like the following screenshot. Press the left arrow key to rewind the song, and click anywhere on the sketch window to move the playhead. You can use the Space bar to pause/resume the song.

How it works...

If you want to use the `minim` library, you always need to have a `Minim` object, with a reference to the main `PApplet` class. Playing audio files is done with the `AudioPlayer` class. You need to load the audio file into the `AudioPlayer` object, using the following code:

```
player = minim.loadFile("song.mp3");
```

Playing the audio file can be done with the `player.play()` method, which will play the audio file only once. If you want to play the song again and again, you can use the `player.loop()` method.

We've also added a little keyboard interface to control the playback for the audio file. If you press the Space bar, the audio file will be paused or resumed. I've used the `player.isPlaying()` method to check if the audio file is currently playing. This method returns a boolean value. If it returns `true`, playback of the audio is paused with the `player.pause()` method, and if it returns `false` the song starts playing again from the point where it was paused before. If you press the left arrow key, the song will start all over again. This is done by using the `player.rewind()` method.

Inside the `draw()` function, we've used two methods to draw the playhead. The `player.length()` method returns an integer value, which is the length of the audio file in milliseconds. The `player.position()` method returns the current location of the playhead, within the song. We've used the `map()` function to convert the current playhead position to a value between 0 and the width of our screen, to draw the playhead line. Milliseconds might be a little hard to use as an interface element, since we don't use them on a daily basis to express time, and you'll need to convert them to minutes and seconds. This is done with the following lines of code:

```
int seconds = (int)(milliseconds/1000) % 60;
int minutes = (int)(milliseconds/(1000*60)) % 60;
```

In the `mousePressed()` function, we've used the same `length()` and `position()` methods to position the playhead when clicking the mouse. You can use the `play()` method with an integer to start playing the song from a certain point and not from the beginning.

The stop() function is used to close the AudioPlayer object and stop the Minim object. Don't forget to add this function to each sketch where you use the Minim library.

Using live audio

In the *Playing audio files* recipe, you've learned how to play an audio file. This recipe will teach you how to use the microphone input from your computer. This is a great feature of the Minim library and is really easy to use. You can use this as a starting point to build an art installation that responds to sound.

How to do it...

The first thing you need to do is import the minim library, declare a Minim object and an AudioInput object.

```
import ddf.minim.*;
import ddf.minim.signals.*;
import ddf.minim.analysis.*;
import ddf.minim.effects.*;

Minim minim;
AudioInput in;
```

Inside the setup() function, we'll use the getLineIn() method from the Minim class to open the default line-in, on your computer.

```
void setup()
{
  size( 640, 480 );
  smooth();

  minim = new Minim( this );

  in = minim.getLineIn( Minim.STEREO, 512 );

  background( 0 );
}
```

Inside the draw() function, we'll use the bufferSize() method on the AudioInput object to visualize the incoming sound. We'll also add the stop() function to close the line-in, when we quit the sketch.

```
void draw()
{
  fill( 0, 16 );
```

```
  noStroke();
  rect( 0, 0, width, height/2 );

  stroke( 255 );
  noFill();

  float r = 0;
  for ( int i = 0; i < in.bufferSize(); i++ ) {
    r += abs( in.mix.get( i ) ) * 20;
  }

  ellipse( width/2, height/2, r, r );
}

void stop()
{
  in.close();
  minim.stop();
  super.stop();
}
```

Run the sketch and start talking or whistling, to see the result. It will look somewhat like the following screenshot. Depending on your operating system, you may need to enable the microphone of your computer and set it as the default sound input.

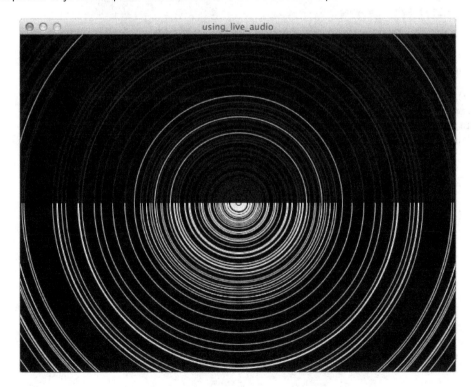

How it works...

The `minim.getLineIn()` method returns an `AudioInput` object. This lets you access the microphone of your computer. You'll most likely use this function with two parameters, but there are more options available. The first parameter is the input type. You can use `Minim.STEREO` for a stereo channel and `Minim.MONO` for a mono channel. The second parameter is the size of the sample buffer; I've used `512`, in this case. If you don't use a second parameter, you'll get a buffer with a size of 1024.

In the `draw()` function, I've used the `bufferSize()` method to loop through the audio buffer and calculate the radius of the circle. This method returns negative and positive numbers, so I've used the `abs()` function to get rid of the negative numbers. Looping through the audio buffer is usually used to draw waveforms. If you want to know how this works, you should read the next recipe.

Drawing a waveform

If you've used any kind of audio editor before, you'll most likely know that audio is usually displayed as a waveform. In this recipe, we'll take a look at how we can visualize a song by drawing its waveform to the screen.

How to do it...

The first part of this sketch should look familiar. It's basically the same as the sketch you made in the *Playing audio files* recipe.

```
import ddf.minim.*;
import ddf.minim.signals.*;
import ddf.minim.analysis.*;
import ddf.minim.effects.*;

Minim minim;
AudioPlayer player;

void setup()
{
  size( 1024, 480 );
  smooth();

  minim = new Minim( this );

  player = minim.loadFile("song.mp3", 1024);
  player.play();

  strokeWeight( 2 );
}
```

The code that analyses the audio and renders the waveform goes in the `draw()` function. Since our song is a stereo audio file, we'll render the left and right channels in different colors, to the screen. Don't forget to add the `stop()` function at the end of your sketch.

```
void draw()
{
  background( 255 );

  translate( 0, height/2 );

  // right channel
  stroke( 255, 0, 0 );
  for ( int i = 0; i < player.right.size(); i++ ) {
    float y = player.right.get( i ) * 220;
    point( i, y );
  }
  // left channel
  stroke( 0 );
  for ( int i = 0; i < player.left.size(); i++ ) {
    float y = player.left.get( i ) * 220;
    point( i, y );
  }
}

void stop()
{
  player.close();
  minim.stop();
  super.stop();
}
```

If you run the sketch, the result will look like the following screenshot. Alternatively, you could use lines instead of points, to create a more connected wave.

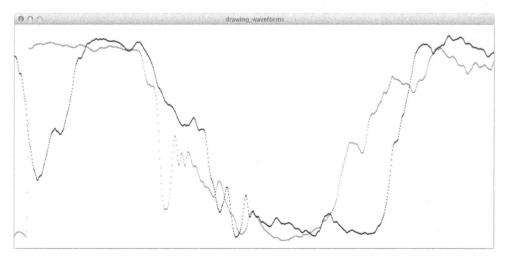

How it works...

The `AudioPlayer` object can return three different waves: one for the left channel, one for the right channel, and a mix of both. You can access them by using the `player.left`, `player.right`, or `player.mix` methods. Using the `size()` method on these objects, you can determine how long the buffer is. This is handy if you need to loop through the buffer. You can get the individual values from this buffer using the `get()` method. These values can be negative or positive and lie between -1 and 1, so you'll need to multiply them with a larger number to make them visible on the screen.

Using Fast Fourier Transforms

Fast Fourier Transforms (**FFT**) are used to visualize the frequency spectrum of an audio file. The Minim library has a class that handles the math for you, so you can focus on drawing the spectrum. If you want to learn more about Fast Fourier Transforms, you should read this paper by *Paul Bourke*, available at `http://paulbourke.net/miscellaneous/dft/`. While you are on his website, check out the rest of the things Paul has done. You'll find some really amazing geometry algorithms.

How to do it...

The first part of this sketch is similar to the previous ones; the only thing we'll add is an `FFT` object with the same buffer size and sample rate as the song we'll load.

```
import ddf.minim.*;
import ddf.minim.signals.*;
import ddf.minim.analysis.*;
import ddf.minim.effects.*;

Minim minim;
AudioPlayer player;
FFT fft;

void setup()
{
  size( 1024, 480 );

  minim = new Minim( this );

  player = minim.loadFile("song.mp3", 512 );
  player.loop();

  fft = new FFT( player.bufferSize(), player.sampleRate() );

  background( 255 );
}
```

In the `draw()` function, we'll loop through the `fft` buffer and draw each frequency band to the screen. I didn't use the `background()` function here, since I wanted to add a fading effect to show the history of the frequency spectrum. This fading effect can be done by setting the fill color to a very low opacity and drawing a rectangle with the same dimensions as the window.

```
void draw()
{
  fill( 255, 8 );
  noStroke();
  rect( 0, 0, width, height );

  fft.forward( player.mix );

  strokeWeight( 4 );
  strokeCap( SQUARE );
  stroke( 0 );

  for ( int i = 0; i < fft.specSize(); i++ ) {
    line( i*4, height, i*4, height - fft.getBand( i ) * 20 );
  }
}

void stop()
{
  player.close();
  minim.stop();
  super.stop();
}
```

The result of the sketch looks like the following screenshot. You'll see that the song we're using has many low frequencies and few high frequencies.

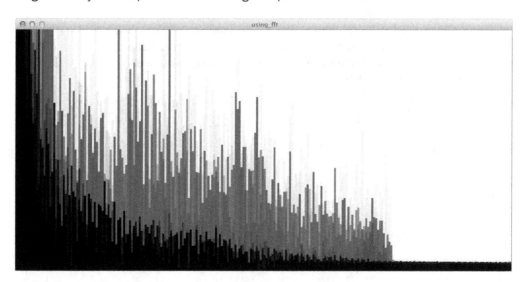

How it works...

To use FFT, you need to create an FFT object with the same buffer size and sample rate as your audio player. You can pass the values of the AudioPlayer object into the constructor, using the following code:

```
fft = new FFT( player.bufferSize(), player.sampleRate() );
```

Inside the draw() function, you need to do a forward transform on the buffer, using the following line of code. I've used both channels, but you can also use the player.left or player.right methods, if you want to visualize the audio spectrum of the two channels separately.

```
fft.forward( player.mix );
```

To draw the frequency bands to the screen, you need to loop through the FFT object, using the fft.specSize() method. The size of this spectrum is calculated in the FFT object as *player.bufferSize() / 2 + 1*. You can get the value of each frequency band, using the fft.getBand() method. Since these values are small, you also need to multiply them with a number so you'll see them on the screen.

Audio reactive particles

In this recipe, we'll take a look at how we can create interesting audio reactive visuals. This sketch might be a good start, if you want to create your own software to do performances. This sketch is similar to the FFT example, but the visual output is a lot more interesting.

How to do it...

We'll start by importing the minim library and will declare a Minim object, an AudioPlayer object, and an FFT object. We also need an array to store our Particle objects and a boolean variable to use the fading effect or to draw a background in each frame. This is the code for the first part of the sketch.

```
import ddf.minim.*;
import ddf.minim.signals.*;
import ddf.minim.analysis.*;
import ddf.minim.effects.*;

Minim minim;
AudioPlayer player;
FFT fft;

Particle[] particles;

boolean fade = false;
```

```
void setup()
{
  size( 640, 480 );
  smooth();

  background( 0 );

  colorMode( HSB, 360, 100, 100, 100 );

  minim = new Minim( this );

  player = minim.loadFile("song.mp3", 512 );
  player.loop();

  fft = new FFT( player.bufferSize(), player.sampleRate() );

  particles = new Particle[ fft.specSize() ];
  for ( int i = 0; i < fft.specSize(); i++ ) {
    particles[i] = new Particle( i );
  }
}
```

The draw() function looks a little different from the FFT example. I've used the pushStyle() and popStyle() combo to switch to the RGB color mode, so that we can easily draw the black background or the transparent black rectangle, when fading is enabled. We'll use a for loop to loop through the frequency spectrum, to update and render the particles to the screen.

```
void draw()
{
  pushStyle();
  colorMode( RGB, 255 );
  if ( fade ) {
    noStroke();
    fill( 0, 8 );
    rect( 0, 0, width, height );
  } else {
    background( 0 );
  }
  popStyle();

  fft.forward( player.mix );

  for ( int i = 0; i < fft.specSize() - 1; i++ ) {
    particles[i].update(fft.getBand(i), player.mix.get( i*2 ));
    particles[i].render();
  }
}
```

The next thing you need to do is to add a small interface to toggle the fading. You can do this by adding the `keyPressed()` function to your sketch. As always with Minim, you need to add the `stop()` function to the sketch.

```
void keyPressed()
{
  if ( key == 'f' ) {
    fade = !fade;
  }
}

void stop()
{
  player.close();
  minim.stop();
  super.stop();
}
```

The final thing we'll do is create a `Particle` class. This will allow us to keep track of the location, radius, and color of each particle. Create a new tab using the *Cmd + Shift + N* shortcut on Mac OS X, or *Ctrl + Shift + N* on Windows and Linux, and add the following code.

```
class Particle
{
  PVector loc;
  PVector vel;

  float radius;
  float h;
  float s;
  float b;

  Particle( int id )
  {
    loc = new PVector( map( id, 0, fft.specSize(), 0, width ),
    height/2 );
    vel = new PVector( random( -1, 1 ), random( -1, 1 ) );

    h = map( id, 0, fft.specSize(), 0, 360 );
    s = 100;
    b = 100;
  }

  void update( float _r, float _b )
  {
    loc.add( vel );

    if ( loc.x < 0 || loc.x > width ) {
      vel.x *= -1;
```

```
    }

    if ( loc.y < 0 || loc.y > height ) {
      vel.y *= -1;
    }

    radius = _r;
    radius = constrain( radius, 2, 100 );

    b = map( _b, -1, 1, 0, 100 );
  }

  void render()
  {
    stroke( h, s, b, 50 );
    fill( h, s, b, 20 );
    ellipse( loc.x, loc.y, radius*2, radius*2 );
  }
}
```

If you run the sketch, you'll see the particles move around the screen. Each particle reacts to a different band of the audio spectrum. If you press the *F* key, you can disable/enable the fading effect.

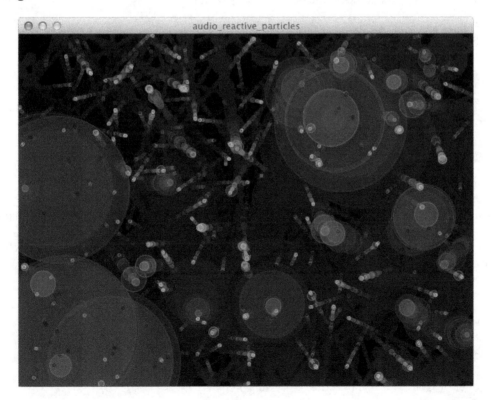

How it works...

The code from the main sketch should be clear to you, if you've made it to this part of the book. The `Particle` class uses some new things, so we'll take a look at how it's constructed. The first things you'll see, right before the constructor, are the variables we need for each `Particle` object. We need a `PVector` object for the location and another one for the velocity of the particle. These will be used to animate the particles. You can learn more about the PVector class at `http://processing.org/reference/PVector.html`. We also need some float variables for the hue, saturation, and brightness—to color the particle—and another one for the radius.

```
PVector loc;
PVector vel;

float radius;
float h;
float s;
float b;
```

The constructor of the `Particle` class takes an integer as a parameter. This integer will be used to set the initial location and color of the particle. I've used a random number between -1 and 1 for the *x* and *y* components of the velocity vector.

```
Particle( int id )
{
  loc = new PVector( map( id, 0, fft.specSize(), 0, width ),
  height/2 );
  vel = new PVector( random( -1, 1 ), random( -1, 1 ) );

  h = map( id, 0, fft.specSize(), 0, 360 );
  s = 100;
  b = 100;
}
```

The `update()` method of the `Particle` class takes two parameters, one to update the radius and one to update the brightness of our particle. These are passed into the object when we loop through the particles in the `draw()` function of our main sketch. The first thing we'll do in the `update()` method is adding the velocity vector to the location vector. Right after that, we'll do a quick check to see if the location of the particle is still inside our sketch window. If the particle goes offscreen, we'll change the *x* or *y* components of the velocity vector, so the particle will bounce against the edges of the window. Finally, the radius and brightness are set from the values coming from the parameters of the method.

```
void update( float _r, float _b )
{
  loc.add( vel );

  if ( loc.x < 0 || loc.x > width ) {
```

```
    vel.x *= -1;
  }

  if ( loc.y < 0 || loc.y > height ) {
    vel.y *= -1;
  }

  radius = _r;
  radius = constrain( radius, 2, 100 );

  b = map( _b, -1, 1, 0, 100 );
}
```

Drawing the particles to the screen is done with the `render()` method. This method sets the stroke and fill color for the particle, and draws an ellipse based on the particle radius.

```
void render()
{
  stroke( h, s, b, 50 );
  fill( h, s, b, 20 );
  ellipse( loc.x, loc.y, radius*2, radius*2 );
}
```

Creating a drum machine

Now that you know how to analyze audio and visualize it, we'll take a look at how we can create instruments. We'll start with building a programmable drum machine with a 16-step sequencer, such as the famous TR-808 and TR-909 drum machines from Roland. You can find out everything about these classic drum machines at Vintage Synth Explorer, at `http://www.vintagesynth.com/roland/808.php`.

How to do it...

You can start by creating an empty sketch and saving it as `drum_machine.pde`. Add a new tab to the sketch and save it as `Button.pde`. We'll write a simple `Button` class so you can toggle buttons on and off. This class will also keep track of playing sounds.

```
class Button
{
  float x;
  float y;
  float w;
  float h;
```

```
boolean isOn;

Button( float _x, float _y )
{
  x = _x;
  y = _y;
  w = 20;
  h = 20;

  isOn = false;
}

void render()
{
  if ( isOn == true ) {
    fill( 255, 0, 0 );
  } else {
    fill( 255 );
  }
  rect( x, y, w, h );
}

void pressButton( int _x, int _y )
{
  if ( _x > x && _x < x + w && _y > y && _y < y + h ) {
    isOn = !isOn;
  }
}
}
```

In the main sketch window, you need to import the `minim` library and declare some variables. I've used the `AudioSample` class instead of the `AudioPlayer` class to load the sounds, because it can be used to trigger samples on command. For each sound, we also need an array with `Button` objects. Inside the `setup()` function, we'll load the sounds and fill the button arrays with a common drum rhythm.

```
import ddf.minim.*;
import ddf.minim.signals.*;
import ddf.minim.analysis.*;
import ddf.minim.effects.*;

Minim minim;
AudioSample samples[];

Button[] bd;
```

```
Button[] sn;
Button[] oh;
Button[] ch;

int playhead;

void setup()
{
  size( 640, 200 );

  minim = new Minim( this );

  samples = new AudioSample[4];
  samples[0] = minim.loadSample( "bd.aif" );
  samples[1] = minim.loadSample( "sn.aif" );
  samples[2] = minim.loadSample( "oh.aif" );
  samples[3] = minim.loadSample( "ch.aif" );

  frameRate( 8 );

  playhead = 0;

  bd = new Button[16];
  for ( int i = 0; i < bd.length; i++ ) {
    bd[i] = new Button( 125 + i * 30, 50 );
    if ( i % 4 == 0 ) {
      bd[i].isOn = true;
    }
  }

  sn = new Button[16];
  for ( int i = 0; i < sn.length; i++ ) {
    sn[i] = new Button( 125 + i * 30, 80 );
    if ( i % 8 - 4 == 0 ) {
      sn[i].isOn = true;
    }
  }

  oh = new Button[16];
  for ( int i = 0; i < oh.length; i++ ) {
    oh[i] = new Button( 125 + i * 30, 110 );
    if ( i % 2 == 1 ) {
      oh[i].isOn = true;
    }
```

```
        }

    ch = new Button[16];
    for ( int i = 0; i < ch.length; i++ ) {
        ch[i] = new Button( 125 + i * 30, 140 );
        if ( i % 2 == 0 ) {
            ch[i].isOn = true;
        }
    }
}
```

In the `draw()` function, we'll start with drawing the playhead for our sequencer, followed by the buttons. Once this is finished, we'll trigger the samples if the button is in the *on* position. Finally, we'll move the playhead to its new position.

```
void draw()
{
    background( 255 );

    // draw playhead
    fill( 0 );
    rect( 120 + playhead * 30, 45, 30, 120 );

    // draw buttons
    fill( 0 );
    text( "*** PROCESSING DRUM MACHINE v1.0 ***", 125, 30 );
    text( "Bassdrum", 20, 65 );
    text( "Snare", 20, 95 );
    text( "Open Hi-hat", 20, 125 );
    text( "Closed Hi-hat", 20, 155 );

    for ( int i = 0; i < bd.length; i++ ) {
        bd[i].render();
    }

    for ( int i = 0; i < sn.length; i++ ) {
        sn[i].render();
    }

    for ( int i = 0; i < oh.length; i++ ) {
        oh[i].render();
    }

    for ( int i = 0; i < ch.length; i++ ) {
        ch[i].render();
```

```
    }

    // play samples
    if ( bd[playhead].isOn ) {
      samples[0].trigger();
    }

    if ( sn[playhead].isOn ) {
      samples[1].trigger();
    }

    if ( oh[playhead].isOn ) {
      samples[2].trigger();
    }

    if ( ch[playhead].isOn ) {
      samples[3].trigger();
    }

    // move playhead
    playhead++;
    if ( playhead >= 16 ) {
      playhead = 0;
    }
  }
```

The `mousePressed()` function is used to toggle the buttons. Each time you click the mouse, we'll loop through all button arrays and use the `pressButton()` method from our `Button` object to check whether the button has been pressed. If this is the case, this method will change the state of the button.

```
void mousePressed()
{
  for ( int i = 0; i < bd.length; i++ ) {
    bd[i].pressButton( mouseX, mouseY );
  }

  for ( int i = 0; i < sn.length; i++ ) {
    sn[i].pressButton( mouseX, mouseY );
  }

  for ( int i = 0; i < oh.length; i++ ) {
    oh[i].pressButton( mouseX, mouseY );
  }
```

```
    for ( int i = 0; i < ch.length; i++ ) {
      ch[i].pressButton( mouseX, mouseY );
    }
  }
```

The last thing we need to do is close all samples and stop the `Minim` object with the `stop()` function.

```
  void stop()
  {
    samples[0].close();
    samples[1].close();
    samples[2].close();
    samples[3].close();
    minim.stop();
    super.stop();
  }
```

If you run the example, you'll see a fully working drum machine. Click the buttons to change the pattern and start composing your own rhythms.

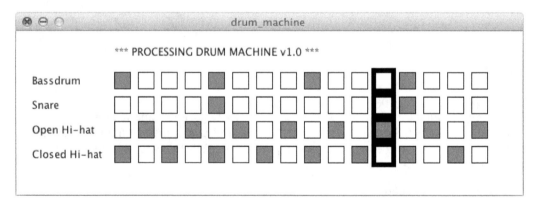

How it works...

We've used the `AudioSample` class instead of the `AudioPlayer` class, in this example. This class is a little different, as it keeps the entire file in memory, and thus should only be used for short samples. This is the ideal format for short drum sounds. To play the file, you need to use the `trigger()` method.

Inside the `setup()` function, I've set the `frameRate` variable of the sketch to 8. If you use a lower number, the drum rhythm will be slower, and if you use a higher number, the rhythm will speed up. This is ok for now, as we only created a very basic instrument. If you want to make a more professional instrument, you'll need to trigger the samples on a time-based interval, which is much harder to implement.

The playhead moves each frame and is set to 0 again if it reaches the last step in our sequencer. The following code checks whether the button for the current playhead position is on and triggers the file when it is on.

```
if ( bd[playhead].isOn ) {
  samples[0].trigger();
}
```

Inside the `Button` class, there is a method named `pressButton()`. This method is triggered on all button arrays, when we press the mouse. The code in the `if` statement is a basic check to see if the `_x` and `_y` points lie within the area of the button. The values of `_x` and `_y` are actually the `mouseX` and `mouseY` variables, passed in via the `mousePressed()` function.

```
void pressButton( int _x, int _y )
{
  if ( _x > x && _x < x + w && _y > y && _y < y + h ) {
    isOn = !isOn;
  }
}
```

Creating a synthesizer

The second instrument we'll create is a synthesizer. We'll use a sine wave and a saw wave to generate an interesting sound. The keyboard will be used to hit notes, and the mouse will pan the sound from left to right.

How to do it...

You need to start by importing the `minim` library and declare a `Minim` object and an `AudioOutput` object. We also need a `SineWave` and a `SawWave` object to generate the sound. In the `setup()` function, we'll create both waves and add them to the output so you'll hear them.

```
import ddf.minim.*;
import ddf.minim.signals.*;
import ddf.minim.analysis.*;
import ddf.minim.effects.*;

Minim minim;
AudioOutput out;
SineWave sine;
SawWave saw;

void setup()
{
```

```
    size( 1024, 480 );
    smooth();

    strokeWeight( 2 );

    minim = new Minim( this );

    out = minim.getLineOut( Minim.STEREO );

    sine = new SineWave( 130.816, 0.5, out.sampleRate() );
    out.addSignal( sine );

    saw = new SawWave( 65.4064, 1.0, out.sampleRate() );
    out.addSignal( saw );
}
```

You'll probably recognize the code inside the `draw()` function. This is more or less the same code that you've used in the *Drawing a waveform* recipe.

```
void draw()
{
  background( 255 );

  translate( 0, height/2 );

  for ( int i = 0; i < out.bufferSize(); i++ ) {
    float y1 = out.left.get( i ) * 100;
    float y2 = out.right.get( i ) * 100;
    stroke( 0 );
    point( i, y1 );
    stroke( 255, 0, 0 );
    point( i, y2 );
  }
}
```

The `mouseMoved()` function is used to pan the sound. When the `mouseX` value is 0, the sine wave will play through the left speaker and the saw wave through the right speaker. When your mouse cursor is at the other side of the window, it will be the other way around.

```
void mouseMoved()
{
  float pan = map( mouseX, 0, width, -1, 1 );
  sine.setPan( pan );
  saw.setPan( -pan );
}
```

The `keyPressed()` function is used to change the frequency of each wave. I've used the second row of keys on my **AZERTY** keyboard, but you can easily change this to any range of keys if you like.

```
void keyPressed()
{
  if ( key == 'q' ) {
    sine.setFreq( 130.813 ); // C3
    saw.setFreq( 65.4064 ); // C2
  }

  if ( key == 's' ) {
    sine.setFreq( 146.832 ); // D3
    saw.setFreq( 73.4162 ); // D2
  }

  if ( key == 'd' ) {
    sine.setFreq( 164.814 ); // E3
    saw.setFreq( 82.4069 ); // E2
  }

  if ( key == 'f' ) {
    sine.setFreq( 174.614 ); // F3
    saw.setFreq( 87.3071 ); // F2
  }

  if ( key == 'g' ) {
    sine.setFreq( 195.998 ); // G3
    saw.setFreq( 97.9989 ); // G2
  }

  if ( key == 'h' ) {
    sine.setFreq( 220 ); // A3
    saw.setFreq( 110 ); // A2
  }

  if ( key == 'j' ) {
    sine.setFreq( 246.942 ); // B3
    saw.setFreq( 123.471 ); // B2
  }
}

void stop()
{
  out.close();
  minim.stop();
  super.stop();
}
```

Run the sketch, press some keys, and move the mouse to create some wonderful tunes.

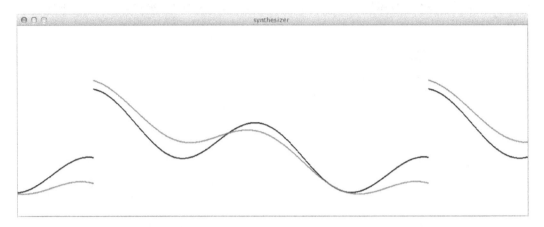

How it works...

The first thing you need to do, if you want to build a synthesizer, is to create an `AudioOutput` object. You can do this with only one line of code:

```
out = minim.getLineOut( Minim.STEREO );
```

Minim has a few different kinds of waves available for you to use. In this example, we've used a sine wave and a saw wave. These constructors take three parameters. The first one is the frequency of the wave, the second one is the amplitude, and the third one is the sample rate. Once you have created these waves, you need to add them as a signal to the AudioOutput example. If you don't do this, you won't hear the sound.

```
sine = new SineWave( 130.816, 0.5, out.sampleRate() );
out.addSignal( sine );
saw = new SawWave( 65.4064, 1.0, out.sampleRate() );
out.addSignal( saw );
```

The `keyPressed()` function is used to change the frequencies of each wave. This is done by using the `wave.setFreq()` method. Every note on a piano keyboard has a specific frequency. If you press the C3 key on a piano, you would generate a tone with a frequency of 130.813Hz. I've used the octave starting with the C3 note for the sine wave, and the octave starting with the C2 note for the saw wave. If you take a look at these numbers, you'll notice that the frequency of the C3 note is equal to the frequency of the C2 x 2. The frequency of the C4 note is also double the C3 frequency, so you can easily calculate the frequency for every note. A full overview of piano notes and their corresponding frequencies can be found on Wikipedia, at http://en.wikipedia.org/wiki/Piano_key_frequencies.

Using effects

In the last recipe of this chapter, you'll learn how to use effects. These effects can be used to shape the waves of a synthesizer you are creating or to change the sound of an audio file.

How to do it...

The beginning of this sketch is the same as that of most of the sketches we've made in this chapter. You'll load an audio file and play it. The only difference is that we'll create a low pass and a high pass filter and add these effects to the `AudioPlayer` object.

```
import ddf.minim.*;
import ddf.minim.signals.*;
import ddf.minim.analysis.*;
import ddf.minim.effects.*;

Minim minim;
AudioPlayer player;

LowPassSP lowpass;
HighPassSP highpass;

void setup()
{
  size( 640, 480 );

  minim = new Minim( this );

  player = minim.loadFile("song.mp3");
  player.play();

  lowpass = new LowPassSP( 440, 44100 );
  player.addEffect( lowpass );

  highpass = new HighPassSP( 440, 44100 );
  player.addEffect( highpass );

}

void draw()
{
  background( 255 );
}
```

```
    void stop()
    {
        player.close();
        minim.stop();
        super.stop();
    }
```

Run the sketch to hear what filters do to your sound. Try commenting the `player.addEffect()` method to hear the difference between a low pass and a high pass filter.

How it works...

To create the filters, you need to declare them before the `setup()` function. I've used a `lowpass` and a `highpass` filter. There are some other filters, such as a `bandpass` filter and a `notch` filter, available in Minim. You can find out more about them in the documentation at `http://code.compartmental.net/minim/javadoc/`. Creating these filters is easy. The high pass and low pass filters take two parameters, one for the frequency, and a second one for the sample rate. Once created, you need to add them to the player using the `player.addEffect()` method.

8

Exploring Computer Vision

In this chapter we will cover:

- ▶ Using a webcam
- ▶ Thresholding video
- ▶ Blob tracking
- ▶ Color tracking
- ▶ Installing the OpenCV library
- ▶ Accessing a webcam with OpenCV
- ▶ Face detection with OpenCV
- ▶ Defining the region of interest with OpenCV
- ▶ Manipulating video with OpenCV

Introduction

You've already learned how you can use standard input devices such as a mouse or a keyboard. In the previous chapter, we used a microphone to visualize audio on the screen. In this chapter, we'll take a look at how we can use a webcam as an input device. Webcams are probably the most ideal devices to use in interactive art installations. They are cheap and can be used to track colors or detect faces.

Using a webcam

The first thing you need to learn is displaying the video from your webcam, on the screen. Processing makes this very easy for you. You'll be up and running in no time, by writing a few lines of code.

How to do it...

The code for this example is really short. You need to start by importing the `video` library that is included with Processing. Go to **Sketch | Import Library | video,** to do this. You also need to declare an object of the `Capture` type. This object will be used to access the webcam on your computer.

```
import processing.video.*;

Capture webcam;
```

Inside the `setup()` function, you need to initialize the `Capture` object with the settings you need and start capturing. In the `draw()` function, we'll draw the current image from the webcam to the screen.

```
void setup()
{
  size( 640, 480 );
  smooth();

  println( Capture.list() );

  webcam = new Capture( this, width, height, 30 );
  webcam.start();
}

void draw()
{
  background( 255 );
  image( webcam, 0, 0 );
}
```

The last function you need to add is, the `captureEvent()` function. This function is called every time a new frame is available.

```
void captureEvent( Capture webcam )
{
  webcam.read();
}
```

If you run the sketch, the result will look like the following screenshot:

How it works...

The first thing you need to do is to initialize the `Capture` object. You can do this with this line of code:

```
webcam = new Capture( this, width, height, 30 );
```

The `Capture()` function can be used with three to five parameters. The first one will always be `this`. The second and third ones are the `width` and `height` of the video. I've used the same width and height as the sketch window, but you can specify a different size as well. In the example, I've used an optional fourth parameter—the frame rate.

If your computer has multiple webcams, you can specify which camera you want to use. You can print all available cameras to the console, using the `Capture.list()` method. You can add the name of the camera as the fourth parameter, like this:

```
webcam = new Capture( this, width, height, "Logitech Camera", 30 );
```

The second thing you need to do is to start capturing frames, using the `start()` method. If you don't do this, nothing will be displayed. In the `draw()` function, you can draw the webcam image to the screen, using the `image()` function.

The `captureEvent()` function is called every time a new frame is available from the webcam. Inside this function, you need to use the `webcam.read()` method to update the webcam image.

Thresholding video

Applying a threshold filter to a webcam feed is a handy technique to use in computer vision. You'll need this to do some basic blob tracking. This technique is very simple. You compare the brightness of every pixel in the webcam feed to a threshold value. Pixels with a higher brightness get a white color, pixels with a lower brightness will be colored black. The end result is an image that consists solely of black and white pixels.

How to do it...

You'll start by importing the `video` library. You've learned how to do this in the *Using a webcam* recipe. Next to our `Capture` object, we also need integer variables named `numPixels` and `threshold`.

```
import processing.video.*;

Capture webcam;

int numPixels;
int threshold;
```

In the `setup()` function, we'll start the webcam, just like in the *Using a webcam* recipe. The `numPixels` variable will be used to store the total number of pixels from the webcam image. This will be handy if we need to loop through them in the `draw()` function. We'll assign an initial value of `127` to the `threshold` variable.

```
void setup()
{
  size( 640, 480 );
  smooth();

  webcam = new Capture( this, width, height, 30);
  webcam.start();

  numPixels = webcam.width * webcam.height;
  threshold = 127;
}
```

Inside the `draw()` function, we'll use the `webcam.available()` method before reading the new image and displaying it on the screen. The code between the `loadPixels()` and `updatePixels()` functions is the threshold algorithm. We'll also draw a red rectangle with white text, to show the current threshold value.

```
void draw()
{
  if ( webcam.available() ) {
    webcam.read();
    image( webcam, 0, 0 );

    loadPixels();
    for ( int i = 0; i < numPixels; i++ ) {
      float b = brightness( webcam.pixels[i] );
      if ( b > threshold ) {
        pixels[i] = color( 255 );
      } else {
        pixels[i] = color( 0 );
      }
    }
    updatePixels();

  }

  fill( 255, 0, 0 );
  noStroke();
  rect( 10, 10, 110, 20 );
  fill( 255 );
  text( "Threshold: " + threshold, 14, 24 );
}
```

The `keyPressed()` function is used as an interface to change the threshold value. The up arrow will increase the threshold value, while the down arrow will decrease it.

```
void keyPressed()
{
  if ( key == CODED ) {
    if ( keyCode == UP ) {
      threshold++;
    }
    if ( keyCode == DOWN ) {
      threshold--;
    }
  }
}
```

Run the sketch and press the up and down arrows to see what happens.

How it works...

You've probably noticed that I didn't use the `captureEvent()` function in this sketch. Inside the `draw()` function, I've used the `webcam.available()` method, which returns a boolean value. The value of this boolean is true if a new frame is available. If you use this method with an `if` statement, the code within this statement will only be executed when a new frame is available. I've read the new image using the `webcam.read()` method and displayed it on the screen with the Processing `image()` function.

The next thing to do is to load the current image from the screen into the pixels array, using the `loadPixels()` function. I've used a `for` loop to loop through the pixel array and compare the brightness of each pixel to the threshold value. If the brightness is greater than the threshold value, the color of the pixel is changed to white. The other pixels are set to black.

```
for ( int i = 0; i < numPixels; i++ ) {
  float b = brightness( webcam.pixels[i] );
  if ( b > threshold ) {
    pixels[i] = color( 255 );
  } else {
    pixels[i] = color( 0 );
  }
}
```

By pressing the up and down arrows, you can change the threshold value. A larger value for the threshold will result in more black pixels, while a smaller value will result in more white pixels. The result of the image will depend a lot on the lighting in the room you are in.

Blob tracking

Now that you know how to apply a thresholding algorithm on a webcam feed, it's time to do some analysis on those pixels. We'll draw a rectangle around all white pixels in the image. This is a very basic brightness tracking algorithm and is useful when you want to create a simple interactive installation with a webcam.

How to do it...

We'll start by importing the `video` library and declaring some variables. We need a `Capture` object to access the webcam and an integer variable to use as a threshold value. The other integer variables are used to track the boundaries around the white pixels in the image.

```
import processing.video.*;

Capture webcam;
int threshold;

int topLeftX;
int topLeftY;
int bottomRightX;
int bottomRightY;

void setup()
{
  size( 640, 480 );

  webcam = new Capture( this, width, height, 30);
  webcam.start();

  threshold = 127;

  topLeftX = width;
  topLeftY = height;

  bottomRightX = 0;
  bottomRightY = 0;
}
```

Inside the `draw()` function, we'll apply the threshold algorithm, just like we did in the *Thresholding video* recipe. We'll loop through the pixel array with a nested `for` loop, because we need to know the exact location of the white pixels, so that we can update the boundary variables. The rest of the code is the same as the threshold video sketch.

```
void draw()
{
  if ( webcam.available() ) {
    webcam.read();
    image( webcam, 0, 0 );

    loadPixels();

    int counter = 0;
    for ( int j = 0; j < webcam.height; j++ ) {
      for ( int i = 0; i < webcam.width; i++ ) {
        color c = webcam.pixels[counter];
        float b = brightness( c );
        if ( b > threshold ) {
          pixels[counter] = color( 255 );
          if ( i < topLeftX ) {
            topLeftX = i;
          }
          if ( j < topLeftY ) {
            topLeftY = j;
          }
          if ( i > bottomRightX ) {
            bottomRightX = i;
          }
          if ( j > bottomRightY ) {
            bottomRightY = j;
          }
        } else {
          pixels[counter] = color( 0 );
        }
        counter++;
      }
    }

    updatePixels();

    noFill();
    stroke( 255, 0, 0 );
    strokeWeight( 2 );
    rect( topLeftX, topLeftY, bottomRightX - topLeftX,
    bottomRightY - topLeftY );

    // reset tracking points
    topLeftX = width;
    topLeftY = height;
```

```
    bottomRightX = 0;
    bottomRightY = 0;

    fill( 255, 0, 0 );
    noStroke();
    rect( 10, 10, 110, 20 );
    fill( 255 );
    text( "Threshold: " + threshold, 14, 24 );
  }
}

void keyPressed()
{
  if ( key == CODED ) {
    if ( keyCode == UP ) {
      threshold++;
    }
    if ( keyCode == DOWN ) {
      threshold--;
    }
  }
}
```

If you run the sketch, you'll see a red rectangle around the white pixels. This algorithm works best in a dark room where you put light on your subject.

How it works...

The tracking algorithm is quite easy. If the brightness of a pixel is greater than the threshold value, we set the pixel to white. In each frame, the values for the top, left-hand side and bottom, right-hand side corner of the boundary box are calculated. Let's take a look at how this works for the top, left-hand side corner.

At the beginning of each frame, the value of the `topLeftX` variable is equal to the width of the sketch window. The `topLeftY` variable is equal to the height of the window. These two variables point to the bottom, right-hand side corner of the sketch window.

```
topLeftX = width;
topLeftY = height;
```

The `for` loop with the `i` counter is used to loop through the horizontal lines of pixels. If the pixel is white, we compare the position to the `topLeftX` value. If it is smaller, we change the value of the `topLeftX` variable. This way, we'll always end up with the x coordinate of the white pixel closest to the left-hand side of the window. The `for` loop with the `j` counter is used to loop through the vertical lines of pixels. We use the same idea to get the y coordinate of the white pixel that is closest to the top of the window. I've used the `min()` function to do this. The following function returns the smallest value for the two variables passed:

```
topLeftX = min( i, topLeftX );
topLeftY = min( j, topLeftY );
```

The `i` and `j` counter variables are also compared to the `bottomRightX` and `bottomRightY` values, to calculate the top, left-hand side corner of the sketch window. But this time, they have to be bigger. I've used the `max()` function to do this. This function does the opposite of the `min()` function and returns the largest number of the two variables you've passed. Once we have found the coordinates we need, we can draw a rectangle around the white pixels with this line:

```
rect( topLeftX, topLeftY, bottomRightX - topLeftX, bottomRightY -
topLeftY );
```

After drawing the rectangle, it's important to set the coordinates of the rectangle to their initial values, so that we can calculate them again for the next video frame.

Color tracking

In the blob tracking example, you've learned a basic brightness tracking algorithm. In this recipe, we'll up the ante and write an algorithm to track colored pixels. This technique will be useful if you want to create an installation that more than one person can interact with. For instance, you can give each participant a brightly colored ball they can use to wave at the camera to control something on the screen.

How to do it...

The code for this example is similar to the blob tracking sketch from the previous recipe. The only difference is that we need a `color` variable named `trackColor` that we'll use to track, and three integer variables, each for its red, green, and blue values. The threshold variable is gone, and we use an integer variable named `maxColorDifference`, instead.

```
import processing.video.*;

Capture webcam;

color trackColor;
int trackR;
int trackG;
int trackB;

int topLeftX;
int topLeftY;
int bottomRightX;
int bottomRightY;

int maxColorDifference;

void setup()
{
  size( 640, 480 );

  webcam = new Capture( this, width, height );
  webcam.start();

  trackColor = color( 255 );
  trackR = (trackColor >> 16) & 0xff;
  trackG = (trackColor >> 8) & 0xff;
  trackB = trackColor & 0xff;
  maxColorDifference = 40;

  topLeftX = width;
  topLeftY = height;

  bottomRightX = 0;
  bottomRightY = 0;
}
```

Inside the draw() function, we'll use a similar technique to the brightness tracking algorithm. Instead of using the brightness() function, we'll separate the color of each pixel into a red, green, and blue value and calculate the distance between those with the dist() function. This distance is then compared to the maxColorDifference variable, so that we can calculate the bounding box around the colored pixels.

```
void draw()
{
  if ( webcam.available() ) {
    webcam.read();
    image( webcam, 0, 0 );

    loadPixels();

    int counter = 0;
    for ( int j = 0; j < webcam.height; j++ ) {
      for ( int i = 0; i < webcam.width; i++ ) {
        color c = webcam.pixels[counter];
        int r = (c >> 16) & 0xff;
        int g = (c >> 8) & 0xff;
        int b = c & 0xff;
        float colorDifference = dist( r, g, b, trackR, trackG,
        trackB );
        if ( colorDifference < maxColorDifference ) {
            if ( i < topLeftX ) {
            topLeftX = i;
          }
            if ( j < topLeftY ) {
            topLeftY = j;
          }
            if ( i > bottomRightX ) {
            bottomRightX = i;
          }
            if ( j > bottomRightY ) {
            bottomRightY = j;
          }
        }
        counter++;
      }
    }

    updatePixels();

    // draw tracking color
    fill( trackColor );
    noStroke();
```

```
    rect( 0, 0, 20, 20 );

    noFill();
    stroke( 0 );
    strokeWeight( 2 );
    rect( topLeftX, topLeftY, bottomRightX - topLeftX,
    bottomRightY - topLeftY );

    // reset tracking points
    topLeftX = width;
    topLeftY = height;
    bottomRightX = 0;
    bottomRightY = 0;
  }
}
```

The `mousePressed()` function is used to set the track color. Hold a brightly colored object in front of the camera, and click on it with the mouse.

```
void mousePressed()
{
  trackColor = webcam.get( mouseX, mouseY );
  trackR = (trackColor >> 16) & 0xff;
  trackG = (trackColor >> 8) & 0xff;
  trackB = trackColor & 0xff;
}
```

If all goes well, you'll see something similar to the following image:

How it works...

The only important difference in the brightness tracking algorithm from the previous recipe is the following piece of code:

```
color c = webcam.pixels[counter];
int r = (c >> 16) & 0xff;
int g = (c >> 8) & 0xff;
int b = c & 0xff;
float colorDifference = dist( r, g, b, trackR, trackG, trackB );
```

We'll take the color of the current pixel, and store it in a variable named c. We separate this color into its red, green, and blue components, with a technique called bit shifting. The line int r = (c >> 16) & 0xff; does the same as int r = red(c) does but is a lot faster. The following lines do the same as the green() and blue() functions. This code is a little hard to read, but it will give your sketch a small speed bump, when you iterate over a lot of pixels. You can learn more about this technique in the Processing reference at http://processing.org/reference/rightshift.html.

The dist() function is usually used to calculate the distance between two points in a 2D or 3D space. I used the red, green, and blue components from the colors as the x, y and z coordinates of a point in a 3D space. The dist() function is used in this case to calculate the difference between the tracking color and the color of the current pixel. The smaller this number, the more similar the colors are. If the value of the colorDifference variable is smaller than the value of the maxColorDifference variable, the color is similar enough to the tracking color and can be used to calculate the bounding box. The algorithm to calculate the top, left-hand side and bottom, right-hand side coordinates of this box is the same as in the brightness tracking example.

Installing the OpenCV library

Until now, we've only used the standard Processing video library to do some basic computer vision. If you want to do some more advanced stuff, such as face recognition, you'll need to use the OpenCV library.

How to do it...

OpenCV for Processing and Java is available for Mac OS X, Windows, and Linux. Everything you need to install the library can be found at http://ubaa.net/shared/processing/opencv/.

The first thing you need to do is install OpenCV. On Windows, you need to download the OpenCV release version 1.0 package and install everything on your computer. For Mac OS X, there is an OpenCV framework 1.1 available. Download the DMG file, open it, and install the package. On Linux, you need to download the OpenCV archive and compile/install everything yourself.

The second step in this process is to download the OpenCV Processing library, unzip it, and drag the folder to your Processing libraries folder. The folder structure should look like the following screenshot:

How it works...

OpenCV (**Open Source Computer Vision**) was originally developed by Intel and is now supported by Willow Garage. The Processing library uses OpenCV 1.0 on Windows and version 1.1 on Mac OS X. These versions were released between 2006 and 2008, which is a long time ago. The current version of OpenCV is 2.3.1, and it has more and better functions. OpenCV 1.0 is written in C. Version 2.0 and later uses C++ and has wrappers for C#, Ruby, and Java. Unfortunately for us, the Processing library works with the older version of OpenCV and not everything is implemented in the library.

The OpenCV library won't work if you run your sketches in 64-bit mode. You need to run your sketches in 32-bit mode for it to work. Go to **Processing | Preferences** and make sure the radio button for **Launch programs** is set to **32-bit mode**.

There's more...

If you really want to use OpenCV 2, you may check out the openFrameworks toolkit at `http://www.openframeworks.cc/`. This is a library for creative coding written in C++. It works in a similar way to Processing, but the learning curve is a little harder.

Accessing a webcam with OpenCV

The first thing we'll do is use the webcam with OpenCV. This will be a little different from using the webcam with the Processing video library.

How to do it...

You need to start by importing the OpenCV library. Go to **Sketch | Import Library | OpenCV**. You'll see that the following line will be imported at the top of your sketch:

```
import hypermedia.video.*;
```

The next thing you need to do is to declare an OpenCV object. In the setup() function, we'll create the object and set up the camera with the capture() method.

```
OpenCV opencv;

void setup()
{
    size( 640, 480 );

    opencv = new OpenCV( this );
    opencv.capture( width, height );
}
```

In the draw() function, we'll read the image from the camera, flip it, and display it using the image() function.

```
void draw()
{
    opencv.read();
    opencv.flip( OpenCV.FLIP_HORIZONTAL );
    image( opencv.image(), 0, 0 );
}
```

The result of the sketch will look like the following screenshot:

How it works...

You'll start by importing the OpenCV library into your sketch. This makes all the functionality of the library available for you to use in your sketch. You need to declare an OpenCV object right before the setup() function, so you can use this object throughout your sketch.

```
import hypermedia.video.*;
OpenCV opencv;
```

In the setup() function, you need to create an instance of the OpenCV class, using the OpenCV constructor. This constructor is used with the this keyword as a parameter and refers to the main PApplet class. The capture() method is used by the openCV object to access the webcam. The first parameter of this method is the width of the video you want to capture, and the second one is the height. I've used the width and height of my Processing sketch, but you can use other numbers.

```
opencv = new OpenCV( this );
opencv.capture( width, height );
```

Inside the `draw()` function, we'll start by using the `read()` method. This method grabs a new frame from the webcam. The `flip()` method is used in this example to mirror the webcam feed. This method can be used with three values: `OpenCV.FLIP_HORIZONTAL`, `OpenCV.FLIP_VERTICAL`, and `OpenCV.FLIP_BOTH`. The `opencv.image()` method returns the current webcam frame as a `PImage` object, which can be displayed on the screen using the standard Processing `image()` function.

```
opencv.read();
opencv.flip( OpenCV.FLIP_HORIZONTAL );
image( opencv.image(), 0, 0 );
```

Face detection with OpenCV

One of the greatest features of OpenCV is that it allows you to do face detection. In this recipe, we'll take a look at how you can do this with a minimum amount of code.

How to do it...

You need to start by importing the OpenCV library, just like you did in previous OpenCV recipes. You also need to import the `java.awt.Rectangle` class, because the face detection algorithm returns rectangle objects. You'll need to type this line yourself, since this is not available from a menu. Inside the `setup()` function, we'll configure OpenCV and use the `cascade()` method to configure how face tracking works.

```
import hypermedia.video.*;
import java.awt.Rectangle;

OpenCV opencv;

void setup()
{
  size( 640, 480 );

  opencv = new OpenCV( this );
  opencv.capture( 320, 240 );
  opencv.cascade( OpenCV.CASCADE_FRONTALFACE_ALT );
}
```

In the `draw()` function, we'll read a new frame from the webcam, flip it, convert it to a grayscale image, and display it on the screen. The `detect()` method is used to detect faces in the image. I've drawn a black rectangle where a face is detected.

```
void draw()
{
  background( 0 );

  opencv.read();
```

```
opencv.flip( OpenCV.FLIP_HORIZONTAL );
opencv.convert( GRAY );
scale( 2 );
image( opencv.image(), 0, 0 );

Rectangle[] faces = opencv.detect();

noStroke();
fill( 0 );
for ( int i = 0; i < faces.length; i++ ) {
  rect( faces[i].x, faces[i].y, faces[i].width, faces[i].height
  );
}
}
```

If you run the sketch, the result should look like the following screenshot:

How it works...

The first thing you need to do is pick a detection method for OpenCV to use with the cascade() method. I've used the OpenCV.CASCADE_FRONTALFACE_ALT haar cascade classifier. This is basically an XML file with a description for OpenCV, so that it can detect faces.

```
opencv.cascade( OpenCV.CASCADE_FRONTALFACE_ALT );
```

There are some other cascades available for you to use if the `CASCADE_FRONTALFACE_ALT` one doesn't work for you. You can also use OpenCV to detect the profile of a face or the body of a person. This is the full list:

- `OpenCV.CASCADE_FRONTALFACE_ALT_TREE`
- `OpenCV.CASCADE_FRONTALFACE_ALT`
- `OpenCV.CASCADE_FRONTALFACE_ALT2`
- `OpenCV.CASCADE_FRONTALFACE_DEFAULT`
- `OpenCV.CASCADE_PROFILEFACE`
- `OpenCV.CASCADE_FULLBODY`
- `OpenCV.CASCADE_LOWERBODY`
- `OpenCV.CASCADE_UPPERBODY`

Face tracking works best on smaller, grayscale images. Large images only slow your sketch down. That's why I've set the webcam size to `320 x 240` pixels, and used `scale(2)` to display everything on the screen.

The `detect()` method checks the current OpenCV image to see if it contains faces. It returns an array of rectangle objects. These rectangle objects can be used to draw something on the screen at the position of the face.

```
Rectangle[] faces = opencv.detect();
```

Defining the region of interest with OpenCV

Sometimes it might be a good thing to let OpenCV know where to search for something. In this recipe, we'll take a look at how we can set the **Region of Interest** (**ROI**). We'll set the ROI to the right part of the screen and use the face detection algorithm from the previous recipe. OpenCV will only be able to detect faces in this region.

How to do it...

The code for this sketch is basically the same as the code from the previous recipe. The only difference is that we use the `ROI()` method in the `draw()` function to set the region of interest.

```
import hypermedia.video.*;
import java.awt.Rectangle;

OpenCV opencv;

void setup()
{
  size( 640, 480 );
```

```
  opencv = new OpenCV( this );
  opencv.capture( 320, 240 );
  opencv.cascade( OpenCV.CASCADE_FRONTALFACE_ALT );
}

void draw()
{
  background( 0 );

  opencv.read();
  opencv.flip( OpenCV.FLIP_HORIZONTAL );
  opencv.convert( GRAY );
  opencv.ROI( 160, 0, 160, 240 );

  scale( 2 );
  image( opencv.image(), 0, 0 );

  Rectangle[] faces = opencv.detect();

  noStroke();
  fill( 0 );
  for ( int i = 0; i < faces.length; i++ ) {
    rect( faces[i].x + 160, faces[i].y, faces[i].width,
    faces[i].height );
  }
}
```

Run the sketch and move your head around. You'll see that your face will only be detected on the right-hand side of the screen.

How it works...

The `ROI()` method sets the region of interest. This method takes four parameters. The first two are the *x* and *y* coordinates for the region. The last two set the width and height of the region. Any OpenCV method called after the `ROI()` method will only be applied to that specific region. This is why face tracking only works on the right-hand side of the screen, in this example.

Manipulating video with OpenCV

In the last recipe of this chapter, we'll take a look at how we can manipulate the incoming video from the webcam. We'll use brightness and contrast filters and blur a part of the image set by the `ROI()` method you've learned about in the previous recipe.

How to do it...

The beginning of the sketch is similar to the ones you've written in previous recipes. You should recognize the following piece of code.

```
import hypermedia.video.*;

OpenCV opencv;

void setup()
{
  size( 640, 480 );

  opencv = new OpenCV( this );
  opencv.capture( width, height );
}
```

In the `draw()` function, we'll use some new methods to change the brightness and contrast of the webcam image. We'll also flip the image so that it appears upside-down and blurs part of the image.

```
void draw()
{
  background( 0 );

  opencv.read();
  opencv.flip( OpenCV.FLIP_BOTH );
  opencv.convert( GRAY );

  opencv.brightness( 20 );
```

```
    opencv.contrast( 80 );

    opencv.ROI( 160, 120, 320, 240 );
    opencv.blur( OpenCV.GAUSSIAN, 41 );

    image( opencv.image(), 0, 0 );
  }
```

The result of the sketch looks like the following screenshot. Play around with the parameters to achieve some different looks.

How it works...

The brightness() method changes the overall brightness of the image. The contrast() method changes the contrast of the image. You can use a number between -128 and 128. Both of these methods can be used in environments with bad lighting to create a better image for tracking.

The blur() method is used to blur the image. The first parameter sets the type of blur. You can use OpenCV.CV_BLUR, OpenCV.CV_GAUSSIAN, OpenCV.CV_MEDIAN or OpenCV.CV_BILATERAL. The second parameter sets the amount of blur; you should use an odd number for this, so that the blur area around each pixel stays symmetrical.

9
Exploring JavaScript Mode

In this chapter we will cover:

- ▶ Creating your first Processing sketch for the Web
- ▶ Creating a custom HTML template
- ▶ Working with fonts
- ▶ Working with images/SVG files
- ▶ Creating 3D sketches for the Web
- ▶ Using Processing.js without the Processing editor
- ▶ Writing sketches with JavaScript
- ▶ Using Processing.js with jQuery
- ▶ Getting started with the Toxiclibs.js library

Introduction

The new JAVASCRIPT mode in Processing 2 uses Processing.js, a JavaScript port of the Processing language. This port uses the HTML5 canvas element to render your Processing sketches. In this chapter, we'll take a look at drawing some simple 2D and 3D sketches with Processing.js. In the more advanced examples, we'll take a look at how we can combine Processing.js with regular JavaScript and the jQuery library.

Creating your first Processing sketch for the Web

In this first recipe, we'll take a look at the new JAVASCRIPT mode. You'll learn about the differences between the STANDARD and the JAVASCRIPT modes.

Getting ready

The first thing you need to do is switch to JAVASCRIPT mode. You already know how to do this, as you've learned about it a while ago. If you can't remember, go take a look at the *Switching modes* recipe in *Chapter 1, Getting Started with Processing 2*.

How to do it...

Once you're in JAVASCRIPT mode, type the following code in the editor. This is just a basic sketch with a line that runs around the screen. You should be able to understand the code.

```
float x, y;
float prevX, prevY;

void setup()
{
  size( 640, 480 );
  smooth();
  background( 0 );

  x = random( width );
  y = random( height );
  prevX = x + random( -10, 10 );
  prevY = y + random( -10, 10 );
}

void draw()
{
  stroke( random( 192 ) );
  strokeWeight( 1 );
  line( x, y, prevX, prevY );

  prevX = x;
  prevY = y;
  x += random( -10, 10 );
  y += random( -10, 10 );
```

```
    if ( x < 0 ) {
      x = width;
    } else if ( x > width ) {
      x = 0;
    }

    if ( y < 0 ) {
      y = height;
    } else if ( y > height ) {
      y = 0;
    }
}
```

If you run the code, you'll notice that your default browser will start up and will show the sketch running inside a webpage. You can see what the sketch looks like in Google Chrome, in the following screenshot:

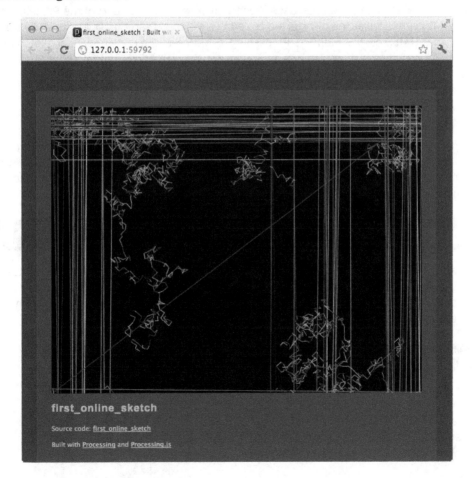

How it works...

When you run this sketch in JAVASCRIPT mode, you'll notice some differences. Processing doesn't compile the code in an executable file, and you won't see your sketch running in a separate window. Instead, Processing starts a web server on an available port, opens your default web browser, and shows a webpage with your sketch. Take a good look at the URL in your browser, it should look like this: 127.0.0.1:59792. The 127.0.0.1 bit is the local IP (Internet Protocol) address for your computer, also known as **localhost**. The part :59792 refers to the port number used to connect to the Web server. Normal web servers usually use port 80. Processing uses a really high number, so it doesn't interfere with the standard web server, if you are running one on your machine.

If you take a look at your sketch folder, you'll see that there is a web-export folder. This folder contains the HTML page, the Processing.js JavaScript file, and the .pde document with your code.

To render your sketch, this webpage uses Processing.js, a JavaScript port of the Processing language. This project was initially started by John Resig, the creator of jQuery, to show the power of the HTML5 canvas element. Processing.js interprets the code from your sketch and uses native JavaScript to draw it to a canvas element. You can find out more about Processing.js on the project's website, at http://processingjs.org/.

There's more...

Since Processing.js is JavaScript-based, it can be used in just about any web application. Sketchpad is an online Processing editor that uses Processing.js. This might be a handy web application to code anywhere you like, even if you don't have Processing installed. You can learn more about Sketchpad at http://sketchpad.cc/.

Creating a custom HTML template

Now that you know how the JAVASCRIPT mode works, it's time to create your own HTML template. This is really handy if you want to take full control of the layout of the web page before showing it on the Internet. The standard HTML might be handy for testing, but it may not be the best way to display your art.

Getting ready

For our template, we'll use the *HTML5 Reset Stylesheet* made by *Richard Clark*. This CSS file will reset margins, paddings, and some other CSS properties, to ensure that you'll have a blank slate to start building your own CSS file. This is a good practice to make sure your website looks the same in every browser. This CSS file can be found at http://html5doctor.com/html-5-reset-stylesheet/.

How to do it...

I won't show you any Processing code in this recipe. You can use the code from the previous recipe. We'll take a look at the HTML and CSS codes we need to create a custom template that you can use for your sketches. To create a new template, go to **JavaScript | Start Custom Template**. Processing will create a `template` folder inside your sketch folder and open it for you. Inside this folder, you'll find two files: `template.html` and `processing.js`. Open the `template.html` file in your favorite text editor, remove the code, and replace it with the following code:

```html
<!DOCTYPE html>
 <head>
  <meta http-equiv="content-type" content="text/html; charset=utf-
   8" />
  <title>@@sketch@@ : Built with Processing and Processing.js
  </title>
  <meta name="Generator" content="Processing" />

  <link rel="stylesheet" href="reset.css" media="screen" />
  <link rel="stylesheet" href="style.css" media="screen" />

  <script src="processing.js" type="text/javascript"></script>
  @@scripts@@
 </head>
 <body>
 <div id="container">
  <div>
  <canvas id="@@id@@" data-processing-sources="@@sketch@@.pde"
   width="@@width@@" height="@@height@@">
    <p>Your browser does not support the canvas tag.</p>
  </canvas>
  <noscript>
    <p>JavaScript is required to view the contents of this
     page.</p>
  </noscript>
  <!--[if lt IE 9]>
    <p>Your browser does not support the canvas tag.</p>
  <![endif]-->
  </div>

  <h1>@@sketch@@</h1>
  <p id="description">@@description@@</p>
  <p id="sources">Source code: @@source@@</p>
```

```
      <p>Built with <a href="http://processing.org"
      title="Processing">Processing</a> and <a
      href="http://processingjs.org"
      title="Processing.js">Processing.js</a></p>
    </div>
    </body>
    </html>
```

You also need to copy the `reset.css` file you've downloaded from the HTML5 doctor website into the `template` folder. The next thing you need to do is to create a new document with your text editor and save it as `style.css` in the `template` folder. This is the CSS code you need to add to the `style.css` file:

```css
body {
  background: #fff;
  color: #000;
  font-family: Helvetica, Arial, sans-serif;
  font-size: 12px;
  line-height: 1.4em;
}

#container {
  width: 640px;
  margin: 40px auto;
}

h1 {
  font-size: 2em;
  line-height: 1em;
  margin-bottom: 0.5em;
}

p {
  margin-bottom: 1.4em;
}

canvas {
  margin-bottom: 30px;
}
```

If you run the sketch in the browser, the result should look like the following screenshot:

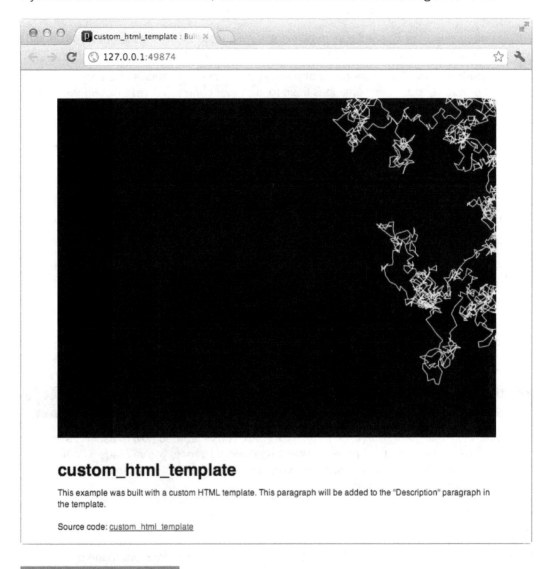

How it works...

If Processing detects a `template` folder in your sketch folder, it will use these files as the template to create the final files for the Web.

The original `template.html` file uses internal CSS, which isn't a good idea. I moved all CSS files to external files, since this is better if you want to reuse your CSS files.

There are a few variables you can use in your HTML template document. When Processing creates the files for the Web, it converts these to their appropriate values.

- `@@scripts@@`: This will add some extra JavaScript to the final document. You should place this variable after loading the `processing.js` file.

- `@@sketch@@`: This is the name of your sketch. In our case, this is `custom_html_template.pde`. This variable is used to load your code so Processing can render it on the canvas element. In this case, it's used on the `data-processing-sources` attribute of the canvas element.

- `@@source@@`: This will be replaced with a link to the original source code of your sketch.

- `@@id@@`: This is used for the ID attribute of the `<canvas>` tag. This is basically the name of your sketch, all lowercase and no special characters.

- `@@width@@` and `@@height@@`: These variables return the width and height of your sketch. You've set these with the `size()` function in your sketch. These can be used to set the width and height of the canvas element.

- `@@description@@`: This variable will be replaced with a description of your sketch. To set this description, you need to add a comment block at the beginning of your sketch. The comment block should look like this:

```
/**
 * This is a short description of the sketch.
 */
```

Working with fonts

In *Chapter 2, Drawing Text, Curves, and Shapes in 2D*, you've learned how to use fonts in your sketches. In JAVASCRIPT mode, you can't use the `.vlw` fonts you've made with the **Create Font** tool. To make fonts work on the web, we'll need a different technique. You'll learn everything you need to know in this recipe.

Getting ready

I've used the Chunk typeface for this example. Chunk is an open source font made by The League of Moveable Type. You can get it from their website, at `http://www.theleagueofmoveabletype.com/chunk`. Download the font, and add the `Chunk.ttf` file to your sketch folder, by dragging it onto the Processing editor.

How to do it...

Once you've added the font to your sketch folder, you can type this code into your editor. The text will scroll from bottom to top, just like in the movies, while a yellow rectangle is animated in the background.

```
PFont font;

float x;
float y;


void setup()
{
  size( 640, 480 );

  font = createFont( "Chunk.ttf", 60 );

  textFont( font );

  x = 0;
  y = height + 60;
}

void draw()
{
  background( 255 );

  noStroke();

  fill( 255, 225, 0 );

  rect( x, 0, random( width/2 ), height );

  String txt = "This is Chunk!";
  float tw = textWidth( txt );

  fill( 0 );
  text( txt, (width-tw)/2, y );

  x += noise( mouseY * 0.02, y * 0.02 );
  if ( x >= width ) {
    x = 0;
```

```
    }

    y--;
    if ( y <= -60 ) {
        y = height + 60;
    }
}
```

If you run the sketch, you'll notice that you can't see the font. This is because we forgot an important step. Go to **JavaScript | Playback Settings (Directives)**, to open the **Directives Editor** dialog box.

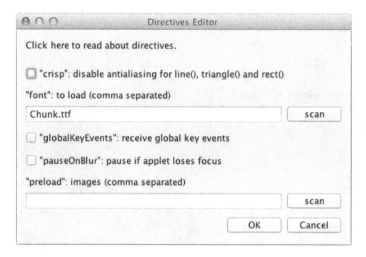

The first text field on this window can be used to make a list of fonts that should be loaded when the sketch runs. If you click on the **scan** button, you'll notice that Chunk.ttf is added to that text field. If you use more than one font, these will also be added, separated with commas. If the **scan** button doesn't find your fonts, you can also add them manually. If you click on the **OK** button, the **Directives Editor** dialog box will close, and the following line will be added to the top of your sketch:

```
/* @pjs font="Chunk.ttf"; */
```

If you run the sketch, you'll see that the font is now rendered on the canvas element.

How it works...

STANDARD mode Processing sketches load the files they need from the `data` folder. But since Processing.js runs in a browser, we need to tell it which files it should request from the server to use in the sketch. That's what the comment on the first line of your sketch is for.

```
/* @pjs font="Chunk.ttf"; */
```

This comment block is called a directive. The `@pjs` part tells Processing.js that everything within this comment block holds instructions for it to use. The `font="Chunk.ttf"` part is an instruction for Processing.js to load the `Chunk.ttf` file from the web server, so that it can be used in the sketch.

There's more...

You can't just use any font with Processing.js; you need to be sure that you have the right to use them. That's why I've used the open source font Chunk, in this example. If you've bought some commercial fonts, chances are that you will not be allowed to use them on the web. You should check the license that comes with the font for this purpose. Some font foundries have special licenses for their fonts, so that you can use them on the web, but you'll have to pay, even if you already bought the font to use it in a desktop publishing environment.

Working with images/SVG files

In this example, we'll take a look at how we can display images and SVG files. You've learned all about this in *Chapter 2, Drawing Text, Curves, and Shapes in 2D*, but just like the fonts example, we'll need to do some extra things to make it work.

Getting ready

Add an image and an SVG file to the `data` folder of your Processing sketch, by dragging them on the Processing editor.

How to do it...

This is the full code for the sketch. We'll just load the image and the SVG file and display them on the canvas element.

```
PImage img;
PShape shapes;

void setup()
{
  size( 640, 480 );

  img = loadImage("osaka-fluo.jpg");

  shapes = loadShape("shapes.svg");

  shapeMode( CENTER );
}

void draw()
```

```
{
  background( 255 );

  image( img, 0, 0 );

  translate( width/2, height/2 );
  shape( shapes, 0, 0 );
}
```

Before you run the sketch, you need to add a directive to preload the image. Go to **JavaScript | Playback Settings (Directives)** and open the **Directives Editor** dialog box. Click on the second **scan** button to add your images to the text field. If you click on **OK**, a directive for loading the images will be added at the top of your sketch. The result of the sketch will look like the following screenshot:

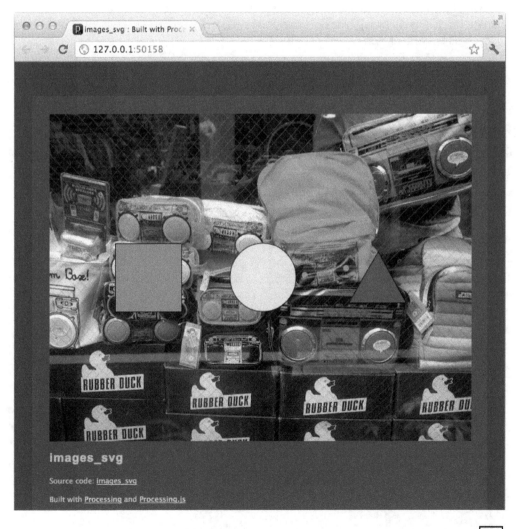

How it works...

The directive to load images works the same way as the one that loads the fonts. You've learned about this in the *Working with fonts* recipe, earlier in this chapter. The directive to load images looks like this:

```
/* @pjs preload="osaka-fluo.jpg"; */
```

If you want to load more images, you can add the file names to this directive, separated by a comma.

There's more...

If you want to load both fonts and images, you can add both the directives to the same comment block. The following block of code shows you how you can load two fonts and three images to use in your sketch.

```
/* @pjs preload="image1.jpg,image2.png,image3.png";
        font="font1.ttf,font2.ttf";
*/
```

Creating 3D sketches for the Web

In this recipe, we'll take a look at the third dimension. Processing.js can be used to display 3D content, so everything that you've learned in *Chapter 3, Drawing in 3D–Lights, Camera, and Action*, can be used on the web.

How to do it...

This is the full code for our 3D sketch. You need to import the OpenGL library and add the OPENGL parameter to the size() function. This sketch will render a yellow box in the middle of the screen. You can manipulate the rotation in the direction of the Y axis by moving your mouse.

```
import processing.opengl.*;

void setup()
{
  size( 640, 480, OPENGL );
  smooth();

  noStroke();
}

void draw()
{
```

```
    background( 255 );

    lights();

    translate( width/2, height/2 );

    rotateX( radians( frameCount ) );
    rotateY( map( mouseX, 0, width, -PI, PI ) );

    fill( 255, 225, 23 );
    box( 200 );
}
```

The sketch looks like the following screenshot when it runs in your browser:

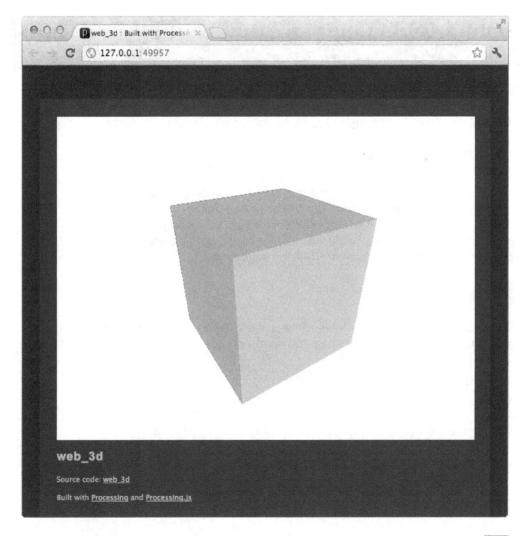

How it works...

The 3D engine that renders your Processing sketch is implemented using WebGL. WebGL is based on OpenGL ES 2.0, a subset of OpenGL. The **ES** in OpenGL ES stands for **Embedded Systems**. This version of OpenGL is used in smartphones and is also implemented in most modern browsers. You can find out more about which browsers are supported, from Wikipedia, at `http://en.wikipedia.org/wiki/WebGL#Desktop_Browsers`.

The only thing you need to do to is import the `OpenGL` library and set the third parameter of the `size()` function to `OPENGL`. Processing.js will actually ignore the import statement, since Java libraries can't be used in `JAVASCRIPT` mode. But, it might be handy to include it if you want to run the sketch in the `STANDARD` mode.

Using Processing.js without the Processing editor

It's time to leave our beloved Processing editor and do something different. We'll take a look at how we can use Processing.js with a regular text editor. This helps you learn about the JavaScript version of Processing and gives you more control over what you do.

Getting ready

Download the latest version of Processing.js at `http://processingjs.org/download/`. You can use the Production version, which is a minified version of the full Development version. The size of this file is a lot smaller, so it is ideal to use on your website. The `Processing.js` file should be placed in the `js` folder. You also need the `reset.css` file we've used in the *Creating a custom HTML template* recipe.

How to do it...

We'll start by creating an HTML file with links to the CSS files and will then include the Processing.js file with a `<script>` tag. This is the full code for the HTML file. You need to save it in a new folder, as `index.html`.

```html
<!doctype html>
<html lang="en">
  <head>
    <meta charset="utf-8" />
    <title>Using Processing.js without the Processing
     editor</title>

    <link rel="stylesheet" href="css/reset.css"
      media="screen" />
```

```
    <link rel="stylesheet" href="css/style.css"
      media="screen" />

  <script src="js/processing-1.3.6.min.js"
    type="text/javascript"></script>
</head>
<body>
  <div id="container">
  <canvas data-processing-
    sources="processingjs_no_editor.pde"></canvas>
  </div>
</body>
</html>
```

The reset.css and style.css files are the same as the ones we've used in the *Creating a custom HTML template* recipe. You need to place them in the css folder, next to the index. html file. You can type the following code in your text editor and save it as processingjs_ no_editor.pde.

```
void setup()
{
  size( 640, 480 );
}

void draw()
{
  background( 225 );
  translate( width/2, height/2 );
  fill( 255, 0, 0 );
  noStroke();
  ellipse( 0, 0, 200, 200 );
}
```

The directory structure for this small website should look like the following screenshot:

Name	Date Modified	Size	Kind
▼ 📁 css	Today 15:34	--	Folder
reset.css	Today 15:34	2 KB	TextW...ument
style.css	Today 15:34	306 bytes	TextW...ument
index.html	Today 15:34	462 bytes	HTML...ument
▼ 📁 js	Today 15:34	--	Folder
processing-1.3.6.min.js	Today 15:34	227 KB	TextW...ument
processingjs_no_editor.pde	Today 15:34	184 bytes	Proces...ce File

If you open the `index.html` file with your browser, the result should look like the following screenshot. If you don't see the sketch, something has gone wrong, but it may not be your fault. Some browsers may have trouble displaying the sketch when you load it locally.

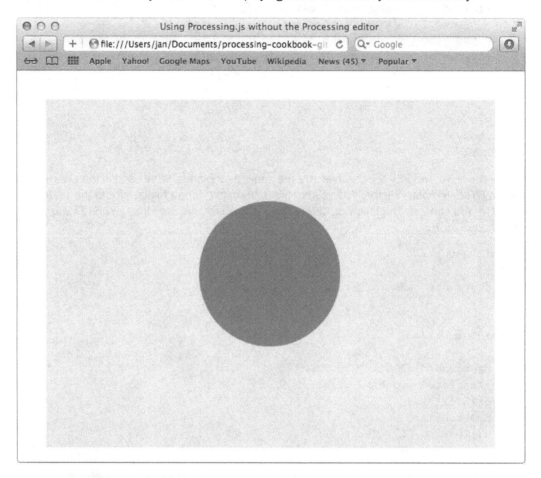

How it works...

The first thing you need to do for your sketches to run is include Processing.js in your HTML document, using the `<script>` tag. This is the line you'll use to do this:

```
<script src="js/processing-1.3.6.min.js" type="text/javascript"></script>
```

The second line of HTML you need is to render a canvas element. In the `data-processing-sources` file, you'll specify the name of your Processing sketch.

```
<canvas data-processing-sources="processingjs_no_editor.pde"></canvas>
```

If you open the HTML file in your browser, you should see the sketch. If you don't see the sketch, there may be a problem with your browser. Firefox and Safari usually don't have problems displaying the sketch when you load it locally. Google Chrome, on the other hand, doesn't display the sketch. If you want to see your sketch with this browser, you'll need to save your files on a web server and surf to the URL.

Writing sketches with JavaScript

Since Processing.js is actually JavaScript, you can use it as a library to write Processing sketches with pure JavaScript. In this recipe, we'll take a look at how you can do this. You'll need the minified Processing.js file you'd downloaded for the previous recipe.

How to do it...

You need to start by creating an HTML file that links the reset.css and style.css files we created in the *Using Processing.js without the Processing editor* recipe. We also need to link the minified Processing.js file and a new JavaScript file named mysketch.js. Note that the <canvas> tag doesn't have a data-processing-sources attribute.

```
<!doctype html>
<html lang="en">
 <head>
  <meta charset="utf-8" />
  <title>Using Processing.js without the Processing editor</title>

    <link rel="stylesheet" href="css/reset.css" media="screen" />
    <link rel="stylesheet" href="css/style.css" media="screen" />

  <script src="js/processing-1.3.6.min.js"
   type="text/javascript"></script>
  <script src="js/mysketch.js"
   type="text/javascript"></script>

 </head>
 <body>
  <div id="container">
   <canvas id="mycanvas"></canvas>
  </div>
 </body>
</html>
```

We won't write any native Processing code in this recipe. Create a new file in your text editor and save it as mysketch.js in the js folder. This is the JavaScript code you'll need to type into that new document:

```
window.onload = function() {
  function mySketch( processing )
```

```
{
  processing.setup = function()
  {
    processing.size( 640, 480 );
    processing.background( 255, 225, 4 );
  }

  processing.draw = function()
  {
    processing.stroke( 0 );
    processing.fill( 0, 64 );
processing.ellipse( processing.random( processing.width ),
 processing.random( processing.height ), 20, 20 );
  }
}

  var canvas = document.getElementById("mycanvas");
  var processingInstance = new Processing( canvas, mySketch );
}
```

If you open the example in your browser, you'll see something like the following screenshot:

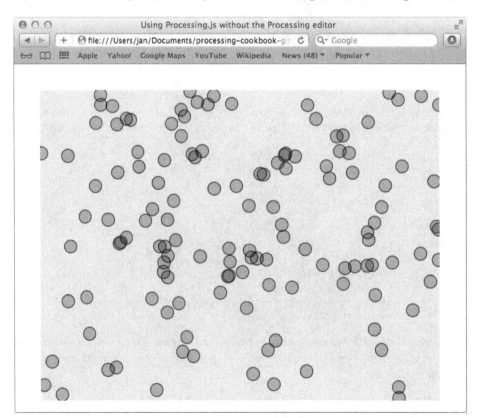

How it works...

The HTML code in this example should be clear to you, as we explained how it works in the previous recipe. We'll take a deeper look at the JavaScript code, because that's where all the magic happens.

```
window.onload = function() {}
```

This first line of code is basically a wrapper around all the other code we need. This function gets executed only when the full page is loaded in the browser. If we don't put all our code between these curly braces, the sketch won't run.

```
function mySketch( processing )
{
  processing.setup = function()
  {
    processing.size( 640, 480 );
    processing.background( 255, 225, 4 );
  }

  processing.draw = function()
  {
    processing.stroke( 0 );
    processing.fill( 0, 64 );
    processing.ellipse( processing.random( processing.width ),
          processing.random( processing.height ), 20, 20 );
  }
}
```

The `mySketch()` function is our actual Processing sketch. We'll pass a reference to the main `processing` variable created by Processing.js. The line `processing.setup() = function() {}` overrides the `setup()` function from Processing.js, so you can define the size of the sketch and some other variables, here. As you may have guessed, the `processing.draw = function() {}` line overrides the `draw()` function, so you can do your custom drawing here. You can use any Processing function inside the `mySketch()` function, as long as you put the `processing` variable in front of it. So, if you want to use `stroke()`, you need to write `processing.stroke()`.

The `document.getElementById()` function returns the canvas element from the DOM tree of the web page as shown in the following code:

```
var canvas = document.getElementById("mycanvas");
```

This last line of code creates a new `Processing` object. You need to pass the `canvas` object and your sketch function to the constructor as shown in the following code:

```
var processingInstance = new Processing( canvas, mySketch );
```

Using Processing.js with jQuery

In this recipe, we'll take a look at how we can combine Processing.js with jQuery. We'll also use jQuery UI (User Interface), a user interface library built on top of jQuery. This library will enable us to use sliders to control our Processing sketch.

Getting ready

Before you start to write code, you need to download jQuery and jQuery UI. You can get everything on the websites for both projects:

- `http://jquery.com/`
- `http://jqueryui.com/`

Place minified jQuery and jQuery UI files in the `js` directory, together with the minified Processing.js file. Add the `reset.css` and `style.css` files to the `css` folder. The base folder you can see in the following screenshot contains CSS files and some images needed for jQuery UI to work properly. You can find the `base` folder inside the `themes` folder of the jQuery UI download file.

Name	Date Modified	Size	Kind
▼ css	Yesterday 18:50	--	Folder
▶ base	Yesterday 18:50	--	Folder
reset.css	Yesterday 18:50	2 KB	Style Sheet
style.css	Yesterday 18:50	495 bytes	Style Sheet
index.html	Yesterday 18:55	905 bytes	HTML...ument
▼ js	Yesterday 18:50	--	Folder
jquery-1.7.2.min.js	Yesterday 18:50	95 KB	TextW...ument
jquery-ui-1.8.18.custom.min.js	Yesterday 18:50	210 KB	TextW...ument
mysketch.js	Yesterday 18:50	1 KB	TextW...ument
processing-1.3.6.min.js	Yesterday 18:50	227 KB	TextW...ument

How to do it...

If all files are in place, it's time to get started. The HTML file looks a little different compared to the one from the *Writing sketches with JavaScript* recipe. I've linked the new CSS and JavaScript files and added a few empty `div` elements that will be used to create the sliders.

```
<!doctype html>
<html lang="en">
 <head>
  <meta charset="utf-8" />
  <title>Using Processing.js with jQuery</title>
```

```
    <link rel="stylesheet" href="css/reset.css"
     media="screen" />
    <link rel="stylesheet" href="css/base/jquery.ui.all.css">
    <link rel="stylesheet" href="css/style.css"
     media="screen" />

    <script src="js/jquery-1.7.2.min.js"
     type="text/javascript"></script>
    <script src="js/jquery-ui-1.8.18.custom.min.js"
     type="text/javascript"></script>

    <script src="js/processing-1.3.6.min.js"
     type="text/javascript"></script>
    <script src="js/mysketch.js"
     type="text/javascript"></script>

  </head>
  <body>
    <div id="container">
     <canvas id="mycanvas"></canvas>

      <p>Use these sliders to change the background color.</p>
     <div id="red"></div>
     <div id="green"></div>
     <div id="blue"></div>

      <p>Use this slider to change the radius of the ball.</p>
     <div id="radius"></div>
    </div>
  </body>
</html>
```

In the CSS file, I've added some selectors to change the appearance of the red, green, and blue sliders. The full CSS code should look like this:

```
body {
  background: #fff;
  color: #000;
  font-family: Helvetica, Arial, sans-serif;
  font-size: 12px;
  line-height: 1.4em;
}

#container {
  width: 640px;
  margin: 40px auto;
}
```

```css
h1 {
  font-size: 2em;
  line-height: 1em;
  margin-bottom: 0.5em;
}

p {
  margin-bottom: 1.4em;
}

canvas {
  margin-bottom: 30px;
}

#red,
#green,
#blue {
  margin-bottom: 20px;
}

#red .ui-slider-range {
  background: #f00;
}

#green .ui-slider-range {
  background: #0f0;
}

#blue .ui-slider-range {
  background: #00f;
}
```

And now, the difficult part—writing the JavaScript code we need to connect the sliders to our Processing sketch:

```javascript
$(document).ready( function() {

  $( "#red, #green, #blue" ).slider({
    orientation: "horizontal",
    range: "min",
    max: 255,
    value: 0,
    slide: updateBackground,
    change: updateBackground
  });

  $( "#radius" ).slider({
```

```
      orientation: "horizontal",
      range: "min",
      min: 40,
      max: 160,
      value: 80,
      slide: updateRadius,
      change: updateRadius
});

var red = 0, green = 0, blue = 0;
var radius = 80;

function updateBackground()
{
  red = $("#red").slider( "value" );
  green = $("#green").slider( "value" );
  blue = $("#blue").slider( "value" );
}

function updateRadius()
{
  radius = $("#radius").slider( "value" );
}

function mySketch( processing )
{
  var x;
  var y;
  var velX = 1;
  var velY = 1;

  processing.setup = function()
  {
    processing.size( 640, 480 );
    processing.background( red, green, blue );
    processing.noStroke();
    processing.fill( 255 );

    x = processing.width/2;
    y = processing.random( processing.height );
  }

  processing.draw = function()
  {
    x += velX;
    if ( x < radius || x > processing.width - radius) {
      velX *= -1;
```

```
      }

      y += velY;
      if ( y < radius || y > processing.height - radius ) {
        velY *= -1;
      }

      processing.background( red, green, blue );
      processing.ellipse( x, y, radius * 2, radius * 2 );
    }
  }

  var canvas = $("#mycanvas")[0];
  var processingInstance = new Processing( canvas, mySketch );
});
```

If all goes well, the end result should look like the following screenshot. The red, green, and blue sliders can be used to change the background color of the sketch; the bottom slider changes the radius of the bouncing ball.

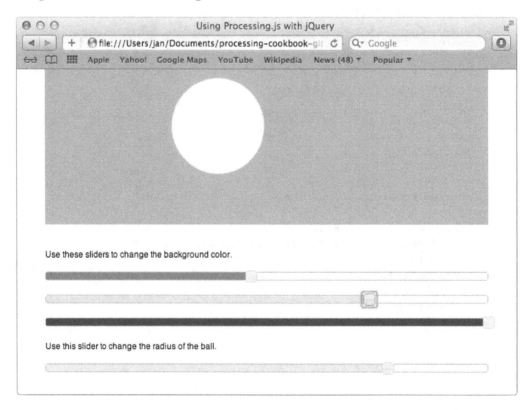

How it works...

Let's break down the JavaScript code into smaller blocks of code, to find out what happens in this sketch.

```
$(document).ready( function() {});
```

This first line is similar to the `window.onload` function in the *Writing sketches with JavaScript* recipe. It's a wrapper function that will only execute once the page has loaded. All your code should go inside the curly braces.

```
$( "#red, #green, #blue" ).slider({
  orientation: "horizontal",
  range: "min",
  max: 255,
  value: 0,
  slide: updateBackground,
  change: updateBackground
});
```

This block of code will create a slider from the empty `div` elements we added to the HTML file. The settings inside the curly braces specify that it will be a horizontal slider, with a maximum value of `255` and an initial value of `0`. The `slide` and `change` settings refer to a callback function named `updateBackground`. The block of code starting with `$( "#radius" ).slider()` will set up the slider that changes the radius of the bouncing ball.

```
var red = 0, green = 0, blue = 0;
var radius = 80;
```

We also need to declare some variables for the red, green, and blue values, and one for the radius. This should be done outside the `mySketch()` function, so that we can access these variables anywhere.

```
function updateBackground()
{
  red = $("#red").slider( "value" );
  green = $("#green").slider( "value" );
  blue = $("#blue").slider( "value" );
}

function updateRadius()
{
  radius = $("#radius").slider( "value" );
}
```

The `updateBackground()` and `updateRadius()` functions are called when the user drags the handle of the slider. In the `updateBackground()` function, we'll assign the current value of the sliders to the red, green, and blue variables. The `updateRadius()` function will change the value of the `radius` variable. If we take a good look at the `draw()` function inside our `mySketch()` function, we'll see that the variables are used to set the background color and draw an ellipse with the radius size.

The last difference is in the way we access the `canvas` object with jQuery. The following line does the same as `document.getElementById()`, which you learned about in the previous recipe:

```
var canvas = $("#mycanvas")[0];
```

Getting started with the Toxiclibs.js library

Toxiclibs, made by *Karsten Schmidt*, is probably the most widely used Processing library. It has some really good classes to work with 2D and 3D geometry, physics, colors, audio, and more. In this recipe, we'll take a look at the JavaScript port made by *Kyle Philips*. You can find out more about `Toxiclibs.js` at `http://haptic-data.com/toxiclibsjs/`.

Getting ready

Before we start coding, you need to download the toxiclibs.js library. You can find it on GitHub, at `https://github.com/hapticdata/toxiclibsjs/`.

Find the `toxiclibs.min.js` file and place it in the `js` folder of a new project. The directory structure for this recipe looks like this:

Name	Date Modified	Size	Kind
▼ 📁 css	Today 16:36	--	Folder
📄 reset.css	Today 16:36	2 KB	TextW...ument
📄 style.css	Today 16:36	306 bytes	TextW...ument
📄 index.html	Today 16:36	529 bytes	HTML...ument
▼ 📁 js	Today 16:39	--	Folder
📄 processing-1.3.6.min.js	Today 16:36	227 KB	TextW...ument
📄 toxiclibs.min.js	Today 16:36	164 KB	TextW...ument
📄 toxiclibs_js.pde	Today 16:36	1 KB	Proces...ce File

How to do it...

The HTML code for this sketch is very straightforward. It just links the `toxiclibs.js` and Processing.js libraries, the CSS files we've used throughout this chapter, and a Processing sketch.

```html
<!doctype html>
<html lang="en">
 <head>
  <meta charset="utf-8" />
  <title>Getting Started with Toxiclibs.js</title>

    <link rel="stylesheet" href="css/reset.css"
     media="screen" />
    <link rel="stylesheet" href="css/style.css"
     media="screen" />

  <script src="js/toxiclibs.min.js"
    type="text/javascript"></script>
  <script src="js/processing-1.3.6.min.js"
    type="text/javascript"></script>

 </head>
 <body>
  <div id="container">
   <canvas id="mycanvas" data-processing-
    sources="toxiclibs_js.pde"></canvas>
  </div>
 </body>
</html>
```

The following is the full code for the Processing sketch. You should recognize most of the code. This example will render four 2D polygons. If you move your mouse over these shapes, their color will change.

```
var Vec2D = toxi.geom.Vec2D,
  ToxiclibsSupport = toxi.processing.ToxiclibsSupport,
  Polygon2D = toxi.geom.Polygon2D;

import toxi.geom.*;
import toxi.processing.*;

ToxiclibsSupport gfx;
Polygon2D[] polygons;

void setup() {
```

```
    size( 640, 480 );
    smooth();
    noStroke();

    polygons = new Polygon2D[4];
    for ( int j = 0; j < 4; j++ ) {
      int randomNum = floor( random( 3, 8 ) );
      float angle = TWO_PI / randomNum;

      Vec2D[] vertices = new Vec2D[randomNum];
      for ( int i = 0; i < randomNum; i++ ) {
        float x = 100 + (j*150) + cos( i * angle ) * 60;
        float y = height/2 + sin( i * angle ) * 60;
        vertices[i] = new Vec2D( x, y );
      }

      polygons[j] = new Polygon2D( vertices );
    }

    gfx = new ToxiclibsSupport( this );
}

void draw() {
  background( 255, 225, 3 );

  for ( int i = 0; i < 4; i++ ) {
    Vec2D m = new Vec2D( mouseX, mouseY );

    if ( polygons[i].containsPoint( m ) ) {
      fill( 255, 64, 0 );
    } else {
      fill( 0 );
    }
    gfx.polygon2D( polygons[i] );
  }
}
```

If you open the HTML page in your browser, the result will look similar to the following screenshot:

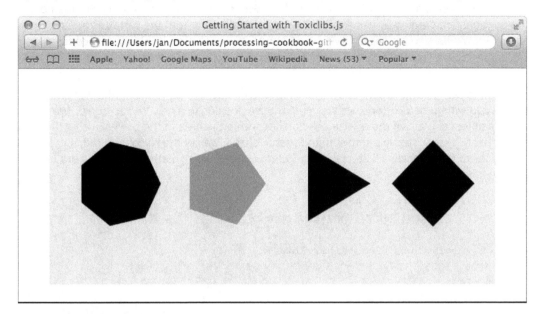

How it works...

The first few lines in the sketch are used to map some of the JavaScript prototypes to the real class names as they would be used in a regular Processing sketch. We do this to make the code compatible with the Java version of Toxiclibs. If you place the following piece of code in a comment block, you can use the sketch within Processing if you've installed Toxiclibs:

```
var Vec2D = toxi.geom.Vec2D,
    ToxiclibsSupport = toxi.processing.ToxiclibsSupport,
    Polygon2D = toxi.geom.Polygon2D;
```

We've also added some import statements for the `toxi.geom` and `toxi.processing` packages. These import statements will be ignored in the JavaScript version but are needed if we want to use the code within Processing.

Right before the `setup()` function, we declared a `ToxiclibsSupport` object and an array to store our `Polygon2D` objects. `ToxiclibsSupport` is a helper class to draw the custom geometry datatypes from Toxiclibs, with Processing.

Inside the setup() function, we used a Vec2D array to store the vertices of our polygon. The Vec2D class is similar to the PVector class from Processing, but it has some extra methods. The polygons are created by using the Polygon2D constructor with the vertex array as a parameter. We've also initialized the ToxiclibsSupport object with this line of code:

```
gfx = new ToxiclibsSupport( this );
```

Inside the draw() function, we use a for loop to draw the four polygons. In the first line of the code within the for loop, we store the mouse position in a new Vec2D object. We use this object to check if the mouse position lies within the area of the polygon using the containsPoint() method. If this method returns true, we set the fill color to red, if it returns false, the fill color will be black. The gfx.polygon2D() method is used to draw the polygon to the screen.

```
for ( int i = 0; i < 4; i++ ) {
  Vec2D m = new Vec2D( mouseX, mouseY );

  if ( polygons[i].containsPoint( m ) ) {
    fill( 255, 64, 0 );
  } else {
    fill( 0 );
  }
  gfx.polygon2D( polygons[i] );
}
```

10
Exploring Android Mode

In this chapter we will cover:

- ▶ Installing the Android SDK
- ▶ Running your sketch in the Android Emulator
- ▶ Running your sketch on an Android device
- ▶ Accessing screen size and density
- ▶ Responding to touch interaction
- ▶ Using the accelerometer
- ▶ Using the GPS
- ▶ Creating 3D sketches on Android
- ▶ Adding an icon to your Android App

Introduction

A few years ago, there was a great initiative called **Mobile Processing**. This was a good starting point to get your Processing sketches to run on cheap Java powered mobile devices, such as cellphones. This project isn't actively developed anymore, because smartphones have gained a lot of the market.

In Processing 2, there is a better method to get your Processing sketches to run on a mobile device: **Android mode**. This new mode enables you to run your sketches in the **Android Emulator** or on an Android device. You can also access the **global positioning system (GPS)** or the **accelerometer** from Processing, and make your sketch react to the touchscreen. In this chapter, we'll take a look at how we can create Android apps with Processing.

Installing the Android SDK

Before we can create Android apps, you need to do some preparations. We'll start by installing the Android SDK on our machine, and tell Processing where to find it. This is the most important step. If we don't do this, we won't be able to use the new Android mode.

How to do it...

The first thing you need to do is point your browser at `http://developer.android.com/sdk/index.html`, and download the **Android Software Development Kit** (**SDK**) for your platform. When the SDK has finished downloading, you need to unzip it, and place it on your hard drive. I've placed it in the `Documents` folder in my home directory.

Go to the `tools` directory in the `android-sdk` folder, and double-click the `android` file. This is a Unix executable file. A terminal window will open, and the Android SDK manager will launch. Check the **Android SDK Platform-tools** and **Android 2.3.3 (API 10)** checkboxes and click the **Install 22 packages...** button, as shown in the following screenshot. Depending on your system, there may be less or more packages to install.

Now that we've installed we need, it's time to launch Processing. In the Processing editor, you need to switch to Android mode. If you don't remember how to do this, take a look at the *Switching modes* recipe from *Chapter 1, Getting Started with Processing 2*, in this book. You'll get an alert window that says Android SDK may not be installed. Click the **Yes** button to move to the next step:

In the file selection window, you need to navigate to the location where you've installed the Android SDK. Select the folder, and click on the **Choose** button.

If everything went well, you are now in Android mode. You'll notice that the color of the Processing editor has changed. It now has a green color scheme.

How it works...

In order to use the Android SDK, Processing needs to know where the SDK is installed. We've installed Android 2.3.3 (API 10), because this is the version Processing will use. You can install newer versions of the API if you need them for regular Android development.

We also went through some steps to locate the Android SDK within Processing. These steps modify your Processing preferences file. On Mac OS X, the file is located in this directory:

```
~/Users/username/Library/Processing/preferences.txt
```

If you open this file in a text editor, you'll find a line that starts with `android.sdk.path`. Processing loads this preferences file when it starts, and uses this line to locate the Android SDK. On Mac OS X, it should look as follows if you've placed the Android SDK in your `Documents` folder:

```
android.sdk.path=/Users/username/Documents/android-sdk-macosx
```

Processing needs the location of the SDK to launch the emulator, or to compile your sketch to a file that can be installed on your device.

Running your sketch in the Android Emulator

Now that you've installed the Android SDK, it's time to get your hands dirty and write some code. We'll start by writing a simple sketch and run it inside the Android Emulator. If you don't have access to an Android device, the emulator is a great application to test your apps.

How to do it...

The code for this app is very straightforward. It leaves a trace of colored circles across the screen. You'll notice that the `size()` function looks a little different. We don't set the dimensions of the sketch window in pixels, as we don't know the screen resolution of the device that our app will run on.

```
float x;
float y;
float prevX;
float prevY;
float d;
float h;

void setup()
{
  size( displayWidth, displayHeight );
  background( 0 );
```

```
    smooth();

    x = random( width );
    y = random( height );
    prevX = x;
    prevY = y;

    stroke( 255, 128 );

    colorMode( HSB, 360, 100, 100, 100 );
}

void draw()
{
  x += random( -30, 30 );
  y += random( -30, 30 );

  x = constrain( x, 0, width );
  y = constrain( y, 0, height );

  d = dist( x, y, prevX, prevY );

  h = map( d, 0, 42, 0, 360 );

  fill( h, 100, 100, 50 );
  ellipse( x, y, d, d );

  prevX = x;
  prevY = y;
}
```

To run your sketch in the Android Emulator, you can click the play button on the Processing IDE, go to the **Sketch | Run in Emulator** menu, or press the *Cmd + R* on your keyboard when you use Mac OS X, or *Ctrl + R* on Windows and Linux. The emulator will start, and run your sketch. This may take a while, as the emulator is rather slow.

 Processing can lose the connection with the emulator if you start your sketch for the first time, so you may have to run it again when the emulator is running.

The result should look as shown in the following screenshot:

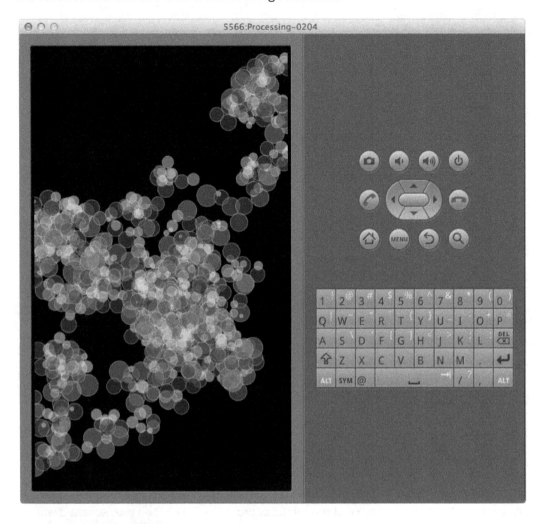

How it works...

Let's start by taking a look at how the `size()` function works in Android mode. In the desktop version we use this function to set the width and height of the window. A third parameter is used to set the rendering mode, either 2D or 3D.

In Android mode, the `size()` function is ignored. But it might be handy to use it as an easy way to set the render mode to 3D. When you run your sketch, the code from your `.pde` file is converted to a `.java` file, and then compiled to an application that can run in the Android Emulator. Let's take a closer look at this piece of code:

```
void setup()
{
   size( displayWidth, displayHeight, P3D );
}
```

When this piece of code is converted to a `.java` file, Processing will convert it to following code:

```
void setup() {}

public int sketchWidth() {
   return displayWidth;
}

public int sketchHeight() {
   return displayHeight;
}

public String sketchRenderer() {
   return P3D;
}
```

The reason why you can't set the size of your sketch is that there are a lot of different Android devices out there. Tablets, top of the line smartphones with a high-resolution screen, and cheap devices with a small screen. So you can't really know where your application will end up. That's why the Android operating system will set the width and height of the sketch for you.

If you take a look at your sketch folder, you'll notice that `sketch.properties` and `AndroidManifest.xml` are added. The `sketch.properties` file is used to tell the Processing editor that it needs to use Android mode for this sketch. The `AndroidManifest.xml` file is required for every Android application and contains entries for things such as permissions.

If you want to stop your sketch, you should press the stop button in the Processing IDE. Don't quit the Emulator. If you make changes to your code, and run it again, it will be installed faster, and you won't have to wait for the Emulator to start up again.

Running your sketch on an Android device

As you are reading this chapter, you probably want to get started with the exciting stuff, and run your sketches on your Android device. The Android Emulator is great for testing, but if you run your app on a real device, you have access to the accelerometer, the GPS, or the touchscreen. Let's take a look at how you can install your sketches on your device.

How to do it...

To run a sketch on your device, you first need to enable USB debugging. To do this, go to **Settings | Applications | Development** on your device, and touch the checkbox next to **USB debugging**:

We'll use the same code as in the previous recipe. Here it is again:

```
float x;
float y;
float prevX;
float prevY;
float d;
float h;

void setup()
{
  size( displayWidth, displayHeight );
  background( 0 );
  smooth();

  x = random( width );
  y = random( height );
  prevX = x;
  prevY = y;
```

```
    stroke( 255, 128 );

    colorMode( HSB, 360, 100, 100, 100 );
}

void draw()
{
  x += random( -30, 30 );
  y += random( -30, 30 );

  x = constrain( x, 0, width );
  y = constrain( y, 0, height );

  d = dist( x, y, prevX, prevY );

  h = map( d, 0, 42, 0, 360 );

  fill( h, 100, 100, 50 );
  ellipse( x, y, d, d );

  prevX = x;
  prevY = y;
}
```

To run your sketch on your device, go to the menu **Sketch | Run on Device**.

How it works...

The first thing you need to do is to enable USB debugging on your device and connect it to your computer with a USB cable. By doing this, you'll be able to use the standard debugging tools that come with the Android SDK to check your apps. This also enables Processing to install sketches on your device. If you choose the **Run on Device** option from the **Sketch** menu, Processing will compile your code, and install it on the device.

Accessing screen size and density

In the *Running your sketch in the Android Emulator* recipe, you've learned that the Android OS sets the size of your sketch window. In this recipe, we'll take a look at how we can access the width, height, DPI, and density values of the screen. There are a lot of Android devices with different screen sizes and resolutions. These values can be used to make your app look good on all of these devices.

Getting ready

I've used the font Junction in this example, an open source font made by The League of Moveable Type. You can download the font from `http://www.theleagueofmoveabletype.com/junction`. Drag the font file `Junction.otf` onto the Processing editor so you can use it in your sketch.

How to do it...

We'll start by importing the Android `DisplayMetrics` class, and declare some String variables and one variable for the font we'll use to display these strings on the screen:

```
import android.util.DisplayMetrics;

String density;
String dpi;
String w;
String h;

PFont junction;
```

Inside the `setup()` function, we'll get the values we need from the `DisplayMetrics` class, and add them to our String variables. We'll also load the Junction font at a size of 32 pixels:

```
void setup()
{
  size( displayWidth, displayHeight );
  smooth();

  DisplayMetrics metrics = new DisplayMetrics();
  getWindowManager().getDefaultDisplay().getMetrics( metrics );

  density = "Density: " + metrics.density;
  dpi = "DPI: " + metrics.densityDpi;
  w = "Width: " + width;
  h = "height: " + height;

  junction = createFont( "Junction.otf", 32 );

  textFont( junction, 32 );

  println( PFont.list() );
}
```

In the `draw()` function, we'll draw our String variables to the screen:

```
void draw()
{
  background( 255, 225, 23 );
  fill( 0 );

  textAlign( CENTER );

  text( density, width/2, 300 );
  text( dpi, width/2, 360 );
  text( w, width/2, 420 );
  text( h, width/2, 480 );
}
```

The sketch looks as shown in the following screenshot, running on an HTC desire smartphone. If you have another device, the values will be different.

Density: 1.5

DPI: 240

Width: 480

height: 800

How it works...

The `DisplayMetrics` class is a general Android class that can access general information about the display of your device. You can initialize this information by declaring a `DisplayMetrics` object as follows:

```
DisplayMetrics metrics = new DisplayMetrics();
getWindowManager().getDefaultDisplay().getMetrics( metrics );
```

After declaring the object, you can access the values you need as in the following piece of code, and use them in your sketch.

```
metrics.density;
metrics.densityDpi;
```

The full overview with accessible fields and methods of the `DisplayMetrics` class can be found at `http://developer.android.com/reference/android/util/DisplayMetrics.html`.

Responding to touch interaction

People have become used to interacting with a device by tapping and swiping on a touchscreen. In this recipe, we'll take a look at how you can detect when a user is touching the screen, and let your sketch respond to that interaction. We'll make a simple drawing application to see how it's done.

How to do it...

We'll start by writing the `setup()` function and declare a boolean variable. If the value of this variable is true, we'll draw some things on the screen.

```
boolean touching = false;

void setup()
{
  size( displayWidth, displayHeight );
  smooth();

  background( 0 );
}
```

To respond to a user touching the screen, we'll override the `surfaceTouchevent()` method. If we detect a touch we'll set the `touching` variable to `true`:

```
public boolean surfaceTouchEvent( MotionEvent event )
{
  if ( event.getAction() == 2 ) {
    touching = true;
  } else {
    touching = false;
  }

  return super.surfaceTouchEvent( event );
}
```

In the `draw()` function, we'll add the `mouseX`, `mouseY`, `pmouseX`, and `pmouseY` system variables to draw circles and lines when the user is touching the screen:

```
void draw()
{
  if ( touching ) {
    stroke( 255, 128 );
    noFill();
    float d = dist( mouseX, mouseY, pmouseX, pmouseY );
    float s = map( d, 0, 200, 1, 10 );
    strokeWeight( s );
    line( mouseX, mouseY, pmouseX, pmouseY );
    fill( 255, 255, 0, 16 );
    stroke( 0, 128 );
    strokeWeight( 1 );
    ellipse( mouseX, mouseY, motionPressure * 100, motionPressure *
100 );
  }
}
```

If you run your sketch on your device, you can start drawing. The result should look as shown in the following screenshot:

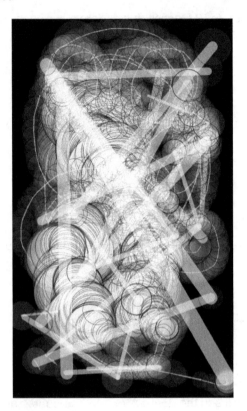

How it works...

Responding to events in Android mode works a little differently than in the Standard mode of Processing. On a desktop computer, you can respond to the keyboard and mouse. These functions are not available on a handheld device. To respond to events, you'll need to override the surfaceTouchEvent() function:

```
public boolean surfaceTouchEvent( MotionEvent event ) {}
```

Inside this function, you can use all methods of the MotionEvent class. The getAction() method returns the type of action being performed on the device as an integer. If this action is equal to 2, you've detected a touch:

```
if ( event.getAction() == 2 ) {
  touching = true;
} else {
  touching = false;
}
```

To make sure everything works properly, we need to call the `super.surfaceTouchEvent()` method in the last line of the function:

```
return super.surfaceTouchEvent( event );
```

Inside the `draw()` function we've used the `motionPressure` variable to set the size of the circles. This variable stores the size of the touch area, and is only updated when the screen is touched.

There's more...

In this recipe, we've only detected a single touch. Most Android devices support multitouch. If you want to use multitouch, there's a simple piece of code to access the data from the screen. In the `surfaceTouchEvent()` function, you need to retrieve the number of touches by calling the `event.getPointerCount()` method. If you loop through these pointer objects, you can easily get the x and y coordinates and the size of the touch. The code looks as follows:

```
public boolean surfaceTouchEvent( MotionEvent event )
{
  int numTouches = event.getPointerCount();

  for ( int i = 0; i < numTouches; i++ ) {
    int touchID = event.getPointerId( i );
    float x = event.getX( i );
    float y = event.getY( i );
    float r = event.getSize( i );
  }
  return super.surfaceTouchEvent( event );
}
```

Using the accelerometer

Most Android devices have an accelerometer. This chip is used to detect the orientation of your device. It will return different values if you hold your device in portrait, landscape, or upside down. In this recipe, we'll take a look at how we can access this chip, and use those values to move a ball across the screen.

Getting ready

Create a new sketch and save it as `accelerometer.pde`. Go to the **File | Examples** menu, search for the **Sensors** folder on this panel, and open the accelerometer example. You'll notice that there is a second tab in this sketch, the `AccelerometerManager.java` class. Copy this file into your new sketch. We'll need it to make our example work.

How to do it...

We'll start by declaring some variables and assigning values to them in the `setup()` function:

```
AccelerometerManager acc;
float ax;
float ay;
float az;
float r;

PVector loc;
color bgcolor;

void setup()
{
  acc = new AccelerometerManager( this );

  size( displayWidth, displayHeight );
  orientation( PORTRAIT );
  smooth();

  loc = new PVector( width/2, height/2 );

  r = 40;

  bgcolor = color( 255, 0, 0 );
}
```

The next thing we'll do is override the `accelerationEvent()` function. This function will be called every time the values of the accelerometer change. We also need to call the `redraw()` function to see the changes:

```
public void accelerationEvent( float x, float y, float z ) {
  ax = x;
  ay = y;
  az = z;
  redraw();
}
```

Inside the `draw()` function, we'll use the `ax` and `ay` variables to change the location of the ball. When the ball hits one of the edges of the screen, we'll change the background color.

```
void draw()
{
  float speedX = - (ax / 2);
  float speedY = ay / 2;

  loc.x += speedX;
  loc.y += speedY;

  if ( loc.x < r ) {
    bgcolor = color( 255, 128, 0, 32 );
  }

    f ( loc.x > width - r ) {
    bgcolor = color( 128, 255, 0, 32 );
  }

  if ( loc.y < r ) {
    bgcolor = color( 0, 225, 255, 32 );
  }

  if ( loc.y > height - r ) {
    bgcolor = color( 255, 0, 128, 32 );
  }

  loc.x = constrain( loc.x, r, width - r );
  loc.y = constrain( loc.y, r, height - r );

  fill( bgcolor );
  rect( 0, 0, width, height );

  fill( 255 );
  noStroke();
  ellipse( loc.x, loc.y, r*2, r*2 );

}
```

Run the sketch on your device and start tilting it. You'll see that the ball will react to gravity, and go to the lowest point. The result should look as shown in the following screenshot:

How it works...

The easiest way to get started using the accelerometer is to use the AccelerometerManager class that comes with the Processing examples. The accelerationEvent() function in the main sketch is used to map the values of the accelerometer to the ax, ay, and az variables.

The first four lines in the draw() function are used to move the ball.

 I inverted the value of ax here to make sure the ball goes in the right direction. I had to do this because the ball was going up when I tilted my device to the left. Depending on your device, you might need to change the ax or ay variables so the ball follows the laws of gravity.

There's more...

If you want better support for using sensors in your Android sketches, there's a great library named Ketai to do those things. You can use the library to add support for the accelerometer, gyroscope, location manager, and cameras to your sketches. You can get it on Google Code: `https://code.google.com/p/ketai/`.

Using the GPS

Most smartphones have a GPS chip. This will enable you to create location-aware applications. In this recipe, we'll take a look at how we can obtain the location of a device, and show it on the screen.

Getting ready

I've used the font Junction in this example, an open source font made by The League of Moveable Type. You can download the font from `http://www.theleagueofmoveabletype.com/junction`. Drag it onto the Processing editor so you can use it in your sketch.

How to do it...

We'll start by importing some of the core android packages, and declare some variables we need to make it work:

```
import android.content.Context;
import android.location.*;
import android.os.Bundle;

LocationManager manager;
GPSLocationListener gps;

float latitude;
float longitude;
float accuracy;
String provider;

PFont junction;
```

The next thing you need to do is to create a new tab, and name it `GPSLocationListener.pde`. We'll write a class in this tab that implements the `LocationListener` interface.

```
class GPSLocationListener implements LocationListener
{
  void onLocationChanged( Location _loc )
  {
    latitude = (float) _loc.getLatitude();
    longitude = (float) _loc.getLongitude();
    accuracy = (float) _loc.getAccuracy();
    provider = _loc.getProvider();
  }

  void onProviderDisabled( String _provider )
  {
    provider = "";
  }

  void onProviderEnabled( String _provider )
  {
    provider = _provider;
  }

  void onStatusChanged( String _provider, int status, Bundle xtras )
  {
  }
}
```

Inside the `setup()` function, we'll set some initial values to our variables, and load the font for displaying the information on the screen:

```
void setup()
{
  orientation( PORTRAIT );

  latitude = 0;
  longitude = 0;
  accuracy = 0;
  provider = "";

  junction = createFont( "Junction.otf", 32 );
  textFont( junction, 32 );
}
```

In the `draw()` function, we'll create a String variable with the latitude, longitude, accuracy, and provider variables. This info will be drawn at the center of the screen:

```
void draw()
{
  background( 5, 10, 85 );
  fill( 250, 255, 13 );
  noStroke();

  translate( width/2, height/2 );

  String msg = "Latitude: " + latitude + "\n";
  msg += "Longitude: " + longitude + "\n";
  msg += "Accuracy: " + accuracy + "\n";
  msg += "Provider: " + provider;

  textAlign( CENTER, CENTER );

  text( msg, 0, 0 );
}
```

We also need to override the `onResume()` and `onPause()` functions to set up the GPS, and read the values:

```
void onResume()
{
  super.onResume();

  gps = new GPSLocationListener();
  manager = (LocationManager) getSystemService( Context.LOCATION_
SERVICE );

    manager.requestLocationUpdates( LocationManager.NETWORK_PROVIDER,
0, 0, gps );
}

void onPause()
{
  super.onPause();
}
```

One last thing you need to do before running your sketch is to make sure that your Android app has permission to access the GPS. Go to the **Android | Sketch Permissions** menu, and check the **ACCESS_FINE_LOCATION** checkbox:

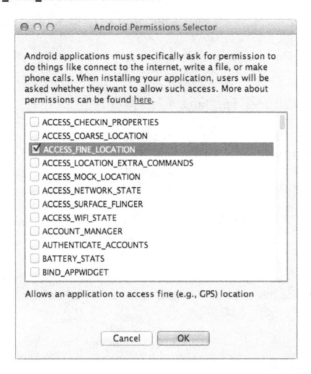

If you run the app on your device, you should see something as shown in the following screenshot. The latitude and longitude values will be different, depending on your location.

How it works...

The `GPSLocationListener` class we wrote implements the Android `LocationListener` interface. An interface in Java is an abstract class, which can't be instantiated. Interfaces have to be implemented in other classes. If you implement an Interface, you have to make sure that you write all methods from the Interface, even if you don't use them. The `LocationListener` interface has four methods: `onLocationChanged()`, `onProviderDisabled()`, `onProviderEnabled()`, and `onStatusChanged()`. In our implementation, the `onStatusChanged()` method does nothing at all, but we need it for our sketch to work. The `onLocationChanged()` method from our class is used to set the values of the `latitude`, `longitude`, `accuracy`, and `provider` variables from our main sketch. The `onProviderDisabled()` and `onProviderEnabled()` methods only change the value of the provider variable.

In the `onResume()` function, we'll create a new `GPSLocationListener` object, set up our `LocationManager` object, and request the location with the following piece of code:

```
manager = (LocationManager) getSystemService( Context.LOCATION_SERVICE
);
  manager.requestLocationUpdates( LocationManager.NETWORK_PROVIDER, 0,
0, gps );
```

There's more...

Note that we actually "cheated" in this example. We are using the **Android Network Location Provider**, which determines the location using cell tower and Wi-Fi signals, rather than the GPS. This is less accurate, but it is faster, uses less battery power, and also works indoors. If you want to access the real GPS, you only need to change `LocationManager.NETWORK_PROVIDER` to `LocationManager.GPS_Provider` to make it work.

Creating 3D sketches on Android

In *Chapter 3, Drawing in 3D–Lights, Camera, and Action!* you've learned everything about drawing stuff in 3D. In this recipe, we'll take a look at how the third dimension works on your Android device.

How to do it...

You can start by typing the following code into a new sketch. The code is very straightforward. It's a white cube and a colorful quad, rotating at the center of the screen.

```
void setup()
{
  size( displayWidth, displayHeight, P3D );
}
```

```
void draw()
{
  background( 0 );

  translate( width/2, height/2, 0 );

  pushMatrix();
  rotateY( radians( frameCount ) );
  fill( 255 );
  noStroke();
  box( 100 );
  popMatrix();

  pushMatrix();
  rotateY( radians( frameCount ) );
  rotateX( radians( frameCount ) );
  beginShape();
  fill( 255, 0, 255 );
  vertex( -200, -200 );
  fill( 0, 255, 0 );
  vertex(  200, -200 );
  fill( 0, 0, 255 );
  vertex(  200,  200 );
  fill( 255, 255, 0 );
  vertex( -200,  200 );
  endShape( CLOSE );
  popMatrix();
}
```

How it works...

As you've learned in the *Running your sketch in the Android Emulator* recipe, the `size()` method is converted to the `sketchWidth()`, `sketchHeight()`, and `sketchRenderer()` functions. If we don't use the `size()` function, the sketch will start with the default 2D renderer. If we use `size( sketchWidth, sketchHeight, P3D );`, the renderer will be set to the 3D renderer. You should be able to use everything you learned in *Chapter 3* on Android. But be careful using complex geometry or lots of particles, as this might slow down your sketch, as your Android device isn't as powerful as your computer.

Adding an icon to your Android App

If you want your app to stand out from the crowd, you'll need a great icon, so people can easily find it on their device. This is probably the easiest recipe from this chapter, but you'll need to know about it if you want to distribute your app via the Android Market.

How to do it...

For this recipe, I made a really conceptual piece of software art, inspired by the visuals of ANBB. It's a red background with a white shape on top of it:

```
void setup()
{
  size( displayWidth, displayHeight );
  smooth();
}

void draw()
{
  // draw red background with white shape.
  background( 255, 0, 0 );

  fill( 255 );
  noStroke();

  beginShape();
  vertex( width/2, 0 );
  vertex( width, height/2 );
  vertex( width/2, height );
  vertex( 0, height/2 );
  endShape( CLOSE );
}
```

The icon I've designed is also red, with the same white shape. Go ahead and create something similar. Fire up your favorite image editor, design an icon of 72 x 72 pixels, and save it as `icon-72.png` in the root of your sketch folder. You also need the same icon at 48 x 48 pixels and at 36 x 36 pixels, and save these files as `icon-48.png` and `icon-36.png`. The folder structure of your sketch should look as shown in the following screenshot:

Name	Date Modified	Size	Kind
adding_icons.pde	Today 17:30	360 bytes	Proces...ce File
AndroidManifest.xml	Today 17:26	615 bytes	Text document
icon-36.png	Today 17:35	529 bytes	Portab...image
icon-48.png	Today 17:35	605 bytes	Portab...image
icon-72.png	Today 17:35	623 bytes	Portab...image
sketch.properties	Today 17:32	13 bytes	Document

If you install your sketch on your device, you'll see that the application now has your icon. I've installed the apps in a folder on my phone, together with some of the other sketches.

How it works...

Android uses the icons of different resolutions, depending on the context they are used in. If your app is on the home screen of your phone, it will use an icon of a different resolution than when it's displayed in a list. The icons should be saved as PNG files with an alpha channel. I didn't use the alpha channel in my icon, because I wanted it to resemble the concept of the application. If you want to create apps to sell, you should probably follow the **Android UI Guidelines**. You can find them at `http://developer.android.com/guide/practices/ui_guidelines/icon_design.html`.

If you don't add icons to your sketch folder, Processing will use the standard icon. If you add all three icons, with the right names, Processing will use these when it compiles your app, and package it to run on your device. The filenames should always be `icon-72.png`, `icon-48.png`, and `icon-36.png`.

 The image files should be in the root directory of your sketch, not in the `data` folder.

11
Using Processing with Other Editors

In this chapter we will cover:

- ▶ Installing Eclipse
- ▶ Installing the Processing plugin for Eclipse
- ▶ Writing your first sketch with the Processing Eclipse plugin
- ▶ Installing the Processing Library Template in Eclipse
- ▶ Writing Processing Libraries
- ▶ Installing the Processing Tool Template
- ▶ Writing Processing tools
- ▶ Using Processing with IntelliJ IDEA

Introduction

The PDE we've used until now is really basic. It doesn't have autocompletion of code or line numbers feature. It's a very good environment for beginners, or if you want to sketch out something really quickly. But if your sketches start growing bigger, and you have a lot of tabs and classes, the PDE might be a little limited. As Processing is based on Java, you can also use it with another IDE. In this chapter we'll take a look at how we can use editors such as Eclipse and IntelliJ IDEA to create Processing sketches, and we'll take a look at how Processing libraries and tools are made.

Installing Eclipse

The first thing you need to do to get started is install **Eclipse**. Eclipse is available for Mac OS X, Windows, and Linux.

Getting ready

Point your browser to http://www.eclipse.org/downloads/ to download Eclipse for your operating system. You'll see that there are a lot of available downloads. There are versions of Eclipse for Java developers, C/C++ developers, JavaScript, and so on. Pick the Eclipse Classic 4.2 version, and download the 32-bit or the 64-bit versions if your operating system supports it.

How to do it...

Once you've downloaded Eclipse, you can extract the contents of the .zip file. Drag the eclipse folder to your Applications folder on Mac OS X, or the Program Files folder on Windows. If you launch Eclipse for the first time, you'll get a message that you need to select a workspace. Eclipse will give you a default location for this folder; you should use this one if you aren't sure what you are doing. If you click **OK**, you'll find a folder named workspace in your Documents directory:

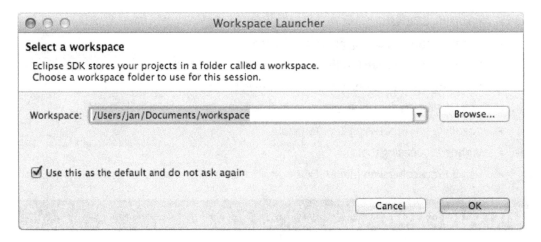

The first thing you'll see after setting up the eclipse workspace is the **Welcome** window, where you'll find an overview of eclipse, and some tutorials and samples. You can click the **Workbench** icon to go to the Eclipse environment. If you ever need the **Welcome** screen again, you can go to the **Help | Welcome** menu.

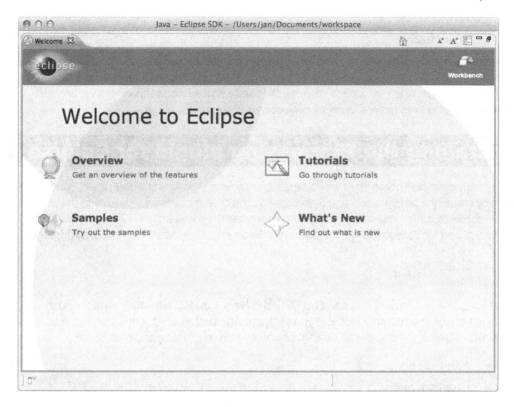

The Eclipse environment looks a lot different than the PDE you've used until now. It might be a little overwhelming at first. But don't worry; we'll take you through the things you need to know when we need them.

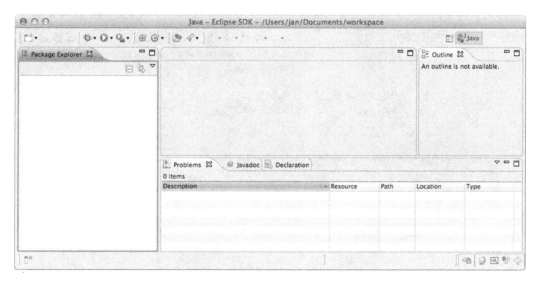

How it works...

When you started Eclipse for the first time, you set the default workspace for Eclipse to work with. This folder has been saved in your `Documents` folder. This workspace folder is where we'll save our files when we create libraries or tools. Eclipse needs this directory, because it also saves some hidden files, such as project metadata and settings.

Installing the Processing plugin for Eclipse

In the early days of Processing, it was a little harder to use Processing with Eclipse. You had to start by creating a Java project, and manually add the core Processing `.jar` file to the project. The Processing team has made it really easy to work with Processing and Eclipse now. They made a plugin for Eclipse that will help you run Processing sketches within the environment.

How to do it...

Start Eclipse if you haven't already, and go to the **Help | Install New Software** menu item. You'll get to see the **Install** window. If you click the **Add** button on this window, the **Add Repository** dialog will show up. Enter these values into this dialog and click on **OK**:

> ▶ **Name**: `Processing Plug-in`
>
> ▶ **Location**: `http://eclipse.processing.org/plugin/site.xml`

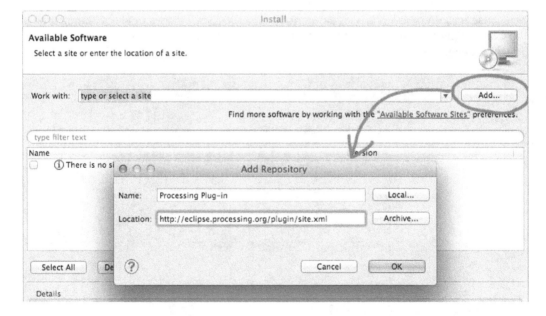

You now get to see the details for the Processing plugin. Click the **Next** button and wait; you'll see a progress bar at the bottom of the window. This process may take a while.

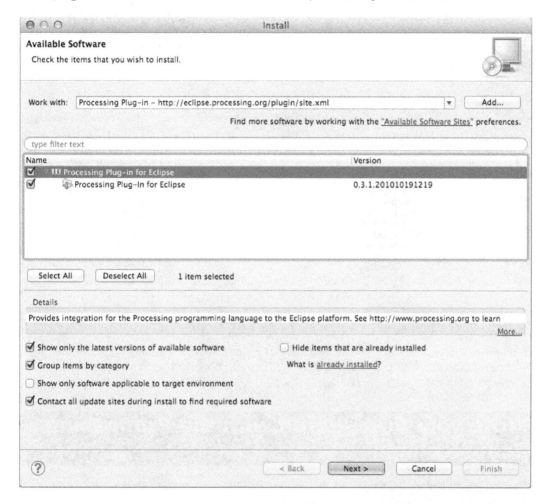

When everything is ready to install, you need to review the license. Click the radio button **I accept the terms of the license agreement**, and click the **Finish** button right after that.

During the install process, you will see a dialog with a security warning. Click **OK** on this window, to continue the installation. Once the installation is complete, you'll have to restart Eclipse to be able to use the Processing plugin.

How it works...

The plugin you've just installed will enable you to write Processing sketches with Eclipse. This plugin consists of several `.jar` files. If you go to the **eclipse** folder in your **Applications**, you'll find a **plugins** folder. At the bottom, you'll find two `.jar` files and a folder with a name that starts with `processing.plugin`.

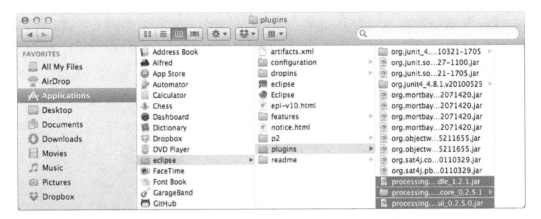

There's more...

While we've used the official Processing plugin for Eclipse, there's another plugin named Proclipsing available. This plugin works a little differently, but offers good integration with Eclipse. You can get it at `http://code.google.com/p/proclipsing/`.

Write your first sketch with the Processing Eclipse plugin

Now that you've installed Eclipse and the Processing plugin, it's time to start writing code. We'll use both to write sketches, just as you would do with the PDE.

How to do it...

The first thing you need to do before you can use the plugin is set up the environment you'll work in. Go to the **Window | Open Perspective | Other...** menu, select **Processing**, and click **OK**. The interface of Eclipse will change a little.

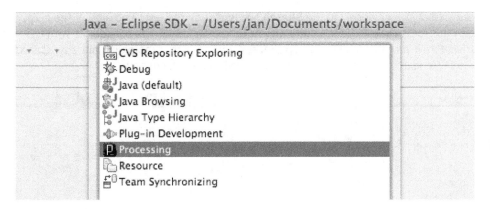

You can now create a new Processing sketch by going to the **File | New | Processing Sketch** menu. You'll get a dialog where you can name your sketch, and pick the sketchbook folder. You should preferably use the default Processing sketchbook, but you can pick another directory if you want. Click the **Finish** button to create the sketch.

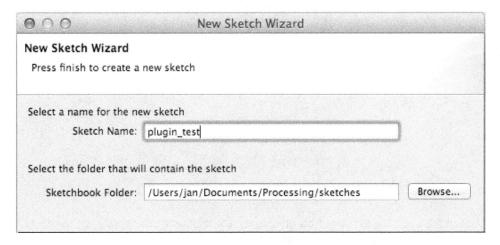

Your new sketch will be added to the **Sketch Navigator** on the left-hand side of the screen. If you open this folder, you'll find the **code** and **data** folders, as well as a .pde file with the name of your sketch. If you double-click the .pde file, it you'll see that the plugin already added some code for you to start with, as shown in the following screenshot:

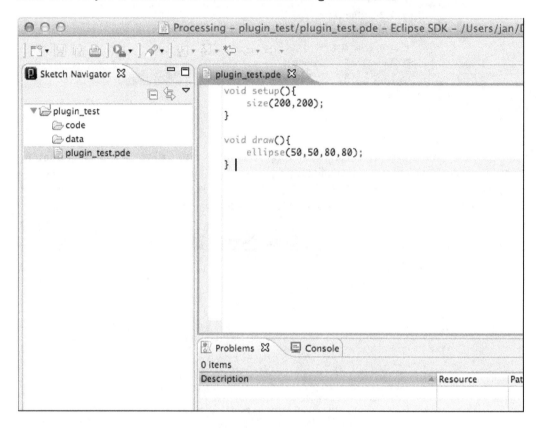

The code in the .pde file will only draw an ellipse, which is quite boring. Change the code in the .pde file to something different. I wrote this little sketch.

```
void setup()
{
  size( 640, 480 );
  smooth();
  background( 0 );
}

void draw()
```

```
{
  float d = random( 20, 40 );
  noFill();
  stroke( 255, 64 );
  ellipse( random( width ), random( height ), d, d );
}
```

To run the sketch, select your `.pde` file in the **Sketch Navigator**, right-click on the sketch, and go to the **Run As | Processing Sketch (Applet)** menu:

The Applet will start, and the result should look as shown in the following screenshot if you've used the same code as I did:

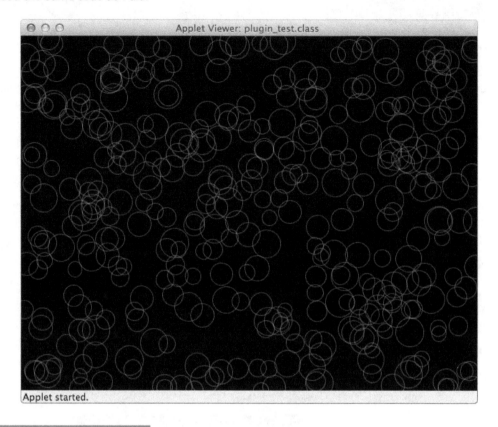

How it works...

When you changed the perspective in Eclipse, you'll have noticed that the interface changed. Eclipse now shows only the things you need to write Processing sketches. The plugin also added a menu item to create a new sketch from the **File** menu, so you can easily start working on new projects, just as you would do in the PDE.

To run the sketch, you had to select the .pde file and select **Run As | Processing Sketch** from the menu. This does the same thing as clicking the play button in the PDE.

There's more...

The **Sketch Navigator** will only show projects that Eclipse is aware of, not all sketches from your sketchbook folder. If you want to work on one of your existing sketches in Eclipse, you can easily import it. Go to the menu **File | Import**, pick the **Import Sketch Wizard** from the **Processing** folder, and click the **Next** button.

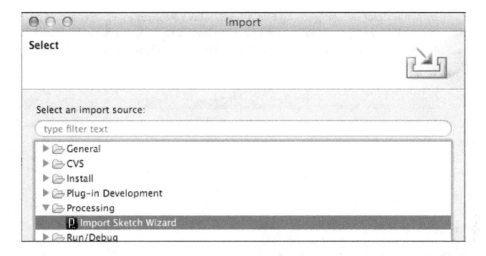

On the **Import Sketch Wizard** dialog, you need to select the sketch folder you want to import. If you click the **Finish** button, your sketch will appear in the **Sketch Navigator**.

Installing the Processing library template in Eclipse

Before we start writing libraries, we need to install the Processing **library template** in Eclipse. This template will help us to package our library so we can easily distribute it to our audience.

Getting ready

Making libraries used to be a little painful, as setting up the project in Eclipse takes some knowledge of the environment and the build process. The Processing team has made a lot of effort in creating a template for Eclipse to streamline this process. You can download the template at `http://code.google.com/p/processing/downloads`, but you don't need to unzip the file.

How to do it...

Now that you've downloaded the Library template, it's time to install it in Eclipse so you can create your own library. If you are still in the Processing perspective, you'll need to switch back to the Java perspective. Go to the **Window | Open Perspective | Other...** menu, select the **Java (default)** perspective, and click the **OK** button.

Create a new Java Project by going to the **File** | **New** | **Java Project** menu. Enter the name of your library in the **Project Name** field. I've named the library `MyLib`. You'll notice that Eclipse will create a directory in your workspace with the name of your library. Click the **Finish** button to create the project.

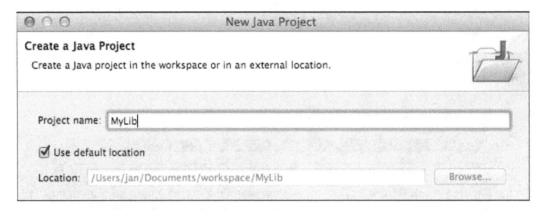

Right-click on the **MyLib** folder, and select **Import...** from the menu. In the **Import** window, select **Archive File** in the **General** folder and click the **Next** button.

Click the **Browse...** button and select the library template `.zip` file you've downloaded. Click the **Finish** button to import all the files from this archive into your project.

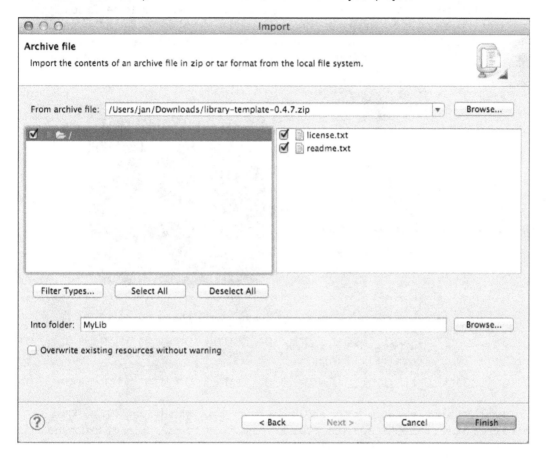

The next thing we need to do is to import the `core.jar` file from Processing to the project. On Windows, you can find this file in the `lib` directory next to the Processing app. On the Mac, you'll need to open the Processing app, because the file is somewhere in there. To do this, select the Processing app in the finder, right-click it, and select **Show Package Contents** in the menu. You'll find the `core.jar` file in the **Contents** | **Resources** | **Java** folder. Select the file, and copy it to your desktop. Don't remove it or the Processing app won't work anymore.

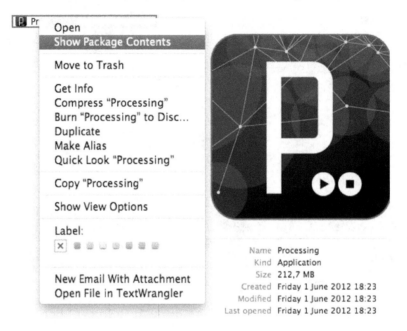

Go to your Eclipse `workspace` folder, and create a new folder with the name `libs`. Drag the `core.jar` file you've copied from your desktop to this folder. Your `workspace` folder should look as shown in the following screenshot:

The next thing we need to do is to add the `core.jar` file to our project. Right-click the **MyLib** folder and select **Properties** from the menu. Select **Java Build Path** in the list on the left-hand side of the window and click the **Libraries** tab at top of the window, just like in the following screenshot. Click the **Add External JARs...** button and select the `core.jar` file from the `/workspace/libs` folder. Click the **Open** button to add the file to your project.

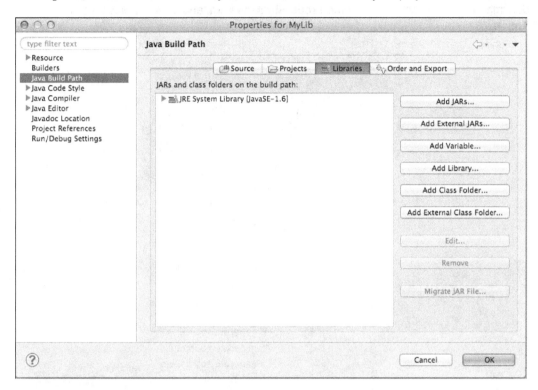

Go to the **resources** folder from your library project in the **Package Explorer**, and double-click the `build.properties` file to open it. This file contains some properties the build process needs to compile the library, and generate the documentation for the library. If you've used the default directories for your Processing sketchbook and Eclipse workspace, you don't need to change a lot of things in this file. Just read through the comments in this file and check if the directories for the `sketchbook.location`, `classpath.local.location`, `classpath.local.include`, and `classpath.libraries.location` are correct. You also need to change your project name to MyLib. You'll find this property under (4) in the document.

```
project.name=MyLib
```

You should also change the properties under (5) in the `build.properties` file. These are used to set some general information for your library such as your name, website, and description of the library.

We've reached the end of this recipe. The library template is installed. There's one more thing we need to do: compile the library to see if everything is ok. Go to the **Window | Show View | Ant** menu. You'll see the **Ant** tab appear on the right-hand side. Drag the `build.xml` file from the `resources` folder of your project onto the **Ant** tab. You'll see a **ProcessingLibs** item appears in the window, which contains all steps needed to compile your library, generate the documentation, and so on. Select the **ProcessingLibs** item, and click the play button on the **Ant** tab.

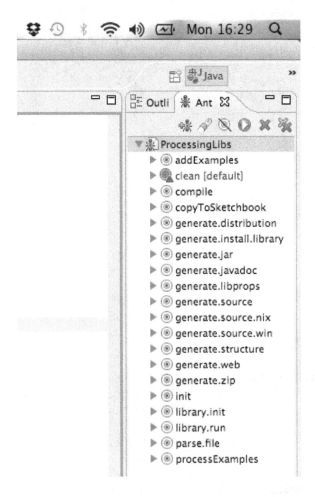

If everything goes well, you'll see a lot of text appearing in the console panel at the bottom of the screen. The last line should be **BUILD SUCCESSFUL**. If this line says **BUILD FAILED**, something went wrong, and you'll have to dig through the messages in the console to figure out the problem.

How it works...

When I first started writing libraries, this template didn't exist. I was using a basic text editor to write code, and the command-line for compiling the files, and had to collect the files manually, and package for distribution. Using Eclipse to make libraries made life a little easier, as you could export your code as a `*.jar` file. This library template takes all those complicated things away, and lets you focus on creating a great library. Let's take a deeper look at what this template does for you.

If you browse your project in the Package Explorer, you'll see a lot of folders. All these folders contain files needed to create the library, and make it ready for distribution. This is what they are used for:

- The **src** folder contains the Java source code for the library.
- The **JRE System Library** folder contains links to the files from the Java Runtime Environment needed to compile our library.
- The **Referenced Libraries** contains a link to the Processing `core.jar` file we've added.
- The **data** folder is used to store images, sounds, or any other file your library may use.
- The **distribution** folder is used to collect everything you need to distribute your library.
- The **examples** folder is used to store example sketches for your library. These examples will be very handy for your users to figure out how they can use your library.
- The **lib** is used to store third party `.jar` files needed by your library, if you've used them.
- The **resources** folder contains some files needed for the build process. You've used the `build.properties` and `build.xml` files in the installation process. The stylesheet.css file is used to make the JavaDoc documentation of your library look good. Standard Java documentation files look really dull.
- The **web** directory contains an html template. This template is used to create a small website for your library, based on the info you've provided under (5) in the `build.properties` file.

If the build process went ok, you'll find the **MyLib** folder inside the distribution folder. When your library is finished, you can upload the contents of this folder to your web server, so people can download the library, and check the documentation and examples.

Writing Processing libraries

Now that you've installed the library template, it's time to get your hands dirty and write some Java. We'll write a small library that can draw hexagons and stars. Nothing fancy, just something small to give you an idea of how libraries are made.

Getting ready

If you haven't installed the Processing library template, you should do this first. The process is explained in the previous recipe, *Installing the Processing library template in Eclipse*.

How to do it...

Go to the **src** directory of your library project in the Package Explorer in Eclipse. You can delete everything in that folder. Select the **src** directory, and go to the **File | New | Class** menu to create a new Java class. In the **package** field, you can type the URL of your website backwards. This will be useful when you import the library into your Processing sketch. In the **Name** field, you can type `MyLib`, the name of the class we'll write. Once you have done this, you can create the new file by clicking the **Finish** button.

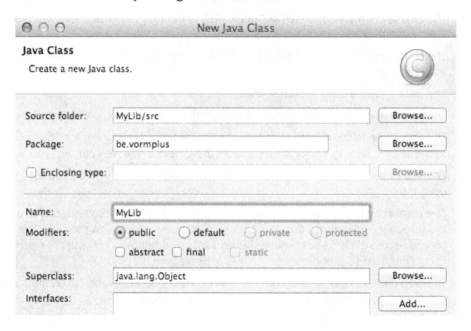

If you open the file, you'll see that Eclipse has added some code:

```
package be.vormplus;
public class MyLib {
}
```

We'll start by importing the Processing core library into our Java class, declare a `PApplet` variable and a `String` variable, and write the constructor for our class. We've imported this library because we're going to use some of Processing's functions in our library. If you don't need to use Processing functions in your library, you don't need to import it. We'll also implement the `PConstants` interface, so we can use the constants defined in Processing. The code should look as follows:

```
package be.vormplus;

import processing.core.*;

public class MyLib implements PConstants {
  PApplet p;

  public final static String VERSION = "##library.prettyVersion##";

  public MyLib( PApplet _p )
  {
    p = _p;
  }
}
```

Our class is almost finished now, we only need to write the methods to draw the hexagon and the star. Type the following code after the constructor:

```
public void drawHexagon( float radius )
{
  p.beginShape();
  for ( int i = 0; i < 6; i++ ) {
    float x = p.cos( i * THIRD_PI ) * radius;
    float y = p.sin( i * THIRD_PI ) * radius;
    p.vertex( x, y );
  }
  p.endShape( CLOSE );
}

public void drawStar( float radius )
{
  float angle = PI / 5;

  p.beginShape();
  for ( int i = 0; i < 10; i++ ) {

    float x, y;

    if ( i % 2 == 0 ) {
      x = p.cos( i * angle ) * radius;
      y = p.sin( i * angle ) * radius;
    } else {
      x = p.cos( i * angle ) * radius/2;
```

```
        y = p.sin( i * angle ) * radius/2;
      }

    p.vertex( x, y );
  }
  p.endShape( CLOSE );
}
```

Now that we've finished writing our little library, it's time to compile. Click the play button on the **Ant** tab, just like you did in the previous recipe. If everything goes well, you should see the **BUILD SUCCESSFUL** message in the console at the bottom of the window. If something went wrong, and you don't see the **BUILD SUCCESSFUL** message, you should read through the error messages in the console. They may help you figure out what went wrong. Eclipse has compiled the library, generated the documentation, and made the little website for our library. During this process, Eclipse also installed a version of the library in the `libraries` folder inside your sketchbook folder. If you open Processing now, you'll see that you can import the `MyLib` library, import it into a new sketch, and type the following code in the PDE:

```
import be.vormplus.*;

MyLib m;

void setup()
{
  size( 640, 480 );
  smooth();

  m = new MyLib( this );
}

void draw()
{
  background( 0 );

  fill( 255, 255, 0 );
  noStroke();

  translate( 200, 240 );
  m.drawHexagon( 100 );

  translate( 240, 0 );
  m.drawStar( 100 );
}
```

If you run the sketch, you should see a black window with two yellow shapes, just like in the following screenshot:

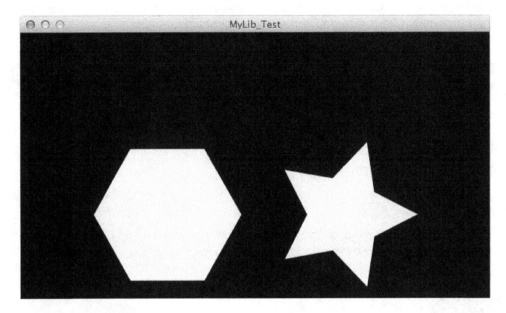

How it works...

We started by creating a new class, and importing the Processing core library. By importing this library, we can use all Processing functions in our library. We also implemented the PConstants interface. By doing this, we can use all constants from Processing, in our library. This is really handy because we need PI, THIRD_PI, and CLOSE to draw our shapes.

If we create a MyLib object in our sketch, we use m = new MyLib(this); in the setup() function. The this keyword is a reference to the main PApplet object. We need to pass this with the constructor so our library can use it. In the constructor, we assign the passed PApplet object (_p) to an internal PApplet object (p).

```
public MyLib( PApplet _p )
{
  p = _p;
}
```

If we want to use Processing functions in our library, we need to call them on the PApplet object. So, if you would use vertex(x, y); in a normal sketch, we need to write p.vertex(x, y); in our library.

When you click the play button on the **Ant** tab, Eclipse compiles your code into a library. It also collects all the files into the right directories, generates documentation, and creates a small website for your library. You'll find everything in the distribution folder of your library project. During this process, Eclipse also installs the library in the libraries folder of your Processing sketchbook. This is really useful, as you can just open Processing, and start testing your library.

Installing the Processing tool template

We've covered installing the library template earlier in this chapter. The Processing team has also made a tool template for Eclipse. This template will let you create **Processing tools** in a more efficient way. In this recipe, we'll take a look at how you can install this template in Eclipse.

Getting ready

You'll need to download the tool template before you can get started with the installation. Download the tool template from `http://code.google.com/p/processing/downloads/list`. You don't have to unzip this file, as we'll import it into our Eclipse project.

How to do it...

You need to start by creating a new Java project in Eclipse. Go to the **File | New | Java Project** menu. Enter the text `MyTool` into the **Project name** text field, and click the **Finish** button.

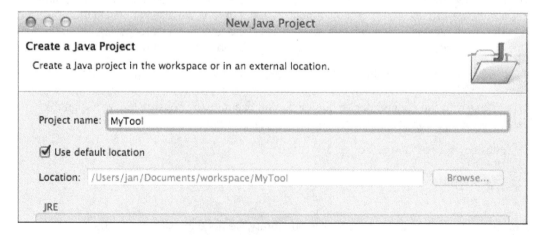

Right-click on the **MyTool** project in the **Package Explorer**, and select **Import...** from the
menu. Select the **Archive File** import source under **General**, and click the **Next** button. Click
the **Browse...** button and select the template tool `.zip` file you've just downloaded. Click on
Finish to import the contents of the file into your project:

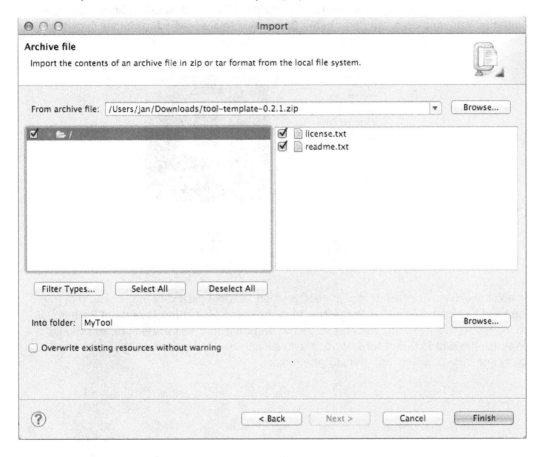

The next thing we need to do is import the `pde.jar` and `core.jar` of Processing into our new project. These `.jar` files should be placed in the `libs` folder of your Eclipse `workspace` folder. On Windows, these `.jar` files can be found in the `lib` directory, next to the Processing app. On the Mac, these files are located within the Processing app, so we'll need to get them out of there. Right-click the Processing app in the **Finder**, and select **Show Package Contents**. You'll find both `.jar` files in the **Contents | Resources | Java** folder. Copy them into the `libs` directory of your Eclipse `workspace` folder.

To add the extra `.jar` files to your project, you need to right-click your project folder in the **Package Explorer**, and select **Properties** from the menu. Select the **Java Build Path** option on the left-hand side of the properties window, and click on the **Libraries** tab. You should now click the **Add External Jars...** button, and select `pde.jar` and `core.jar` from the `libs` folder and click on **OK** to add them to your project.

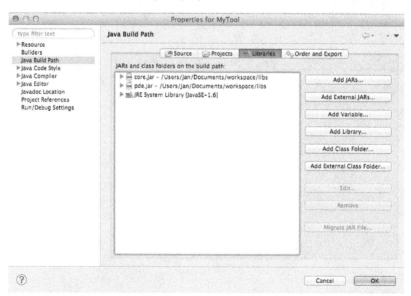

The next thing we'll do is to edit the `build.properties` file you can find in the `resources` folder. All settings will be okay if you've used the default locations for your Processing `sketchbook` and Eclipse `workspace` folders. The only things you need to edit are the project details you'll find under `(4)` and `(5)` at the bottom of the file. Make sure that `project.name` is set to `MyTool`.

The last thing we need to do is open the **Ant** tab by going to the **Window | Show View | Ant** menu. You can drag the `build.xml` file from the `resources` folder onto the **Ant** window. You'll see that this file contains a lot of instructions for Eclipse to compile your tool and create the folders needed for distribution.

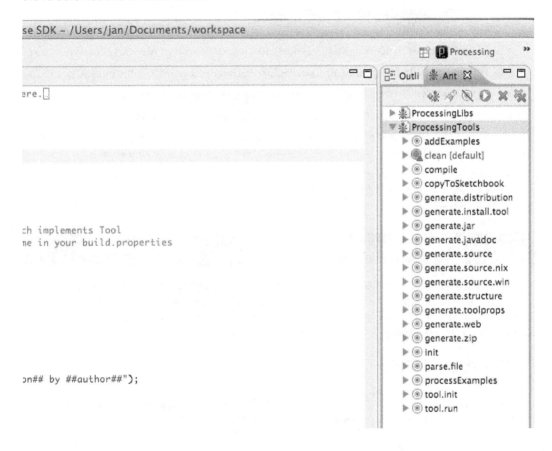

How it works...

If you browse your project in the **Package Explorer**, you'll see a lot of folders. All these folders contain files needed to create our tool, and make it ready for distribution. This project structure is similar to the one from the library template. This is what they are used for:

- The **src** folder contains the Java source code for the Processing tool.
- The **JRE System Library** folder contains links to the files from the Java Runtime Environment needed to compile our Processing tool.
- The **Referenced Libraries** contains links to the Processing `pde.jar` and `core.jar` files we've added.
- The **data** folder is used to store images, sounds, or any other file your tool may use.
- The **distribution** folder is used to collect everything you need to distribute your tool.
- The **examples** folder is used to store example sketches for your tool.
- The **lib**** is used to store third party `.jar` files needed by your tool.
- The **resources** folder contains some files needed for the build process. You've used the `build.properties` and `build.xml` files in the installation process.
- The **web** directory contains an html template. This template is used to create a small website for your Processing tool, based on the info you've provided under (5) in the `build.properties` file.

Writing Processing tools

In this recipe, we'll take a look at how you can create Processing tools. These tools are small applications that can interact with the Processing editor. You can use them to insert code at the caret position, or display a message in the status bar. You can also create extra windows with Java's Swing GUI library. The **Color Selector** tool was made this way.

Getting ready

Before you can start writing code, you need to install the Processing tool template. This is explained in the previous recipe, *Installing the Processing tool template*.

How to do it...

You can start by deleting everything in the `src` directory. We don't need the `HelloTool.java` file, as we are going to write our own class. Select the **src** folder in the **Package Explorer** and go to the **File | New | Class** menu. The name of this file should be `MyTool`.

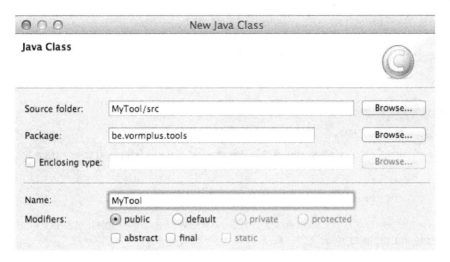

Open the file by double-clicking it. Type the following code into the file, we'll explain everything in the *How it works* section of the recipe.

```
package be.vormplus.tools;

import processing.app.*;
import processing.app.tools.*;

public class MyTool implements Tool {

  Editor editor;

  public void init( Editor _editor )
  {
    editor = _editor;
  }

  public String getMenuTitle()
  {
    return "MyTool";
  }

  public void run()
  {
    String templateCode;
    templateCode  = "void setup() {\n";
    templateCode += "   size( 640, 480 );\n";
    templateCode += "   smooth();\n}\n\n";
    templateCode += "void draw() {\n";
```

```
        templateCode += "    background( 0 );\n}";

        editor.setText( templateCode );
    }
}
```

How it works...

The first thing we did is import some of the Processing classes we need to create a tool:

```
import processing.app.*;
import processing.app.tools.*;
```

Our class implements the `Tool` interface. This means we need to implement all functions that are available in that interface.

```
public class MyTool implements Tool {
    public void init( Editor _editor ) {}
    public String getMenuTitle() {}
    public void run() {}
}
```

Let's take a look at the methods we've implemented in our class:

▸ The `init()` method is called when an editor window first opens. This function is used to assign the Processing `Editor` object passed as a parameter to the internal `Editor` object for our class.

▸ The `getMenuTitle()` method returns the text that you'll see in the **Tools** menu in Processing.

▸ The `run()` method is called when you select the tool from the **Tools** menu. This is the place where you should create a GUI with Swing if your tool requires one.

In our `run()` method, we've created a String that contains some basic Processing code. The `editor.setText()` method is used to replace all text in the current Processing window with our `templateCode` String.

```
public void run()
{
    String templateCode;
    templateCode  = "void setup() {\n";
    templateCode += "    size( 640, 480 );\n";
    templateCode += "    smooth();\n}\n\n\n";
    templateCode += "void draw() {\n";
    templateCode += "    background( 0 );\n}";

    editor.setText( templateCode );
}
```

Once you have finished coding, you can click the play button on the Ant tab. Eclipse will compile your tool, and collect all files in the right folders so you can easily distribute it to your users. It will also install the tool in the tools directory in your Processing sketchbook. If you open Processing, you should see that your tool is available from the Tools menu. If you run it, the template code will be inserted in the PDE.

Using Processing with IntelliJ IDEA

Eclipse isn't the only IDE you can use to create Processing sketches. Just about any environment that supports Java can be used. In this recipe, we'll take a look at how you can use **IntelliJ IDEA** to create Processing sketches. This is a very popular environment for doing Java and Android development.

Getting ready

Before we can get started, you need to download and install the IntelliJ IDEA Community Edition. This is a free version of the IDE. There's also a commercial version available to do advanced Java stuff, but we don't need those features. You can get IntelliJ IDEA right over here: `http://www.jetbrains.com/idea/download/index.html`.

How to do it...

Once you've installed IntelliJ IDEA, it's time to get started and configure our project to write some Processing sketches. We'll start by creating a new project. Go to **File | New Project** to show the new project wizard. Pick the **Create project from scratch** option, and click the **Next** button:

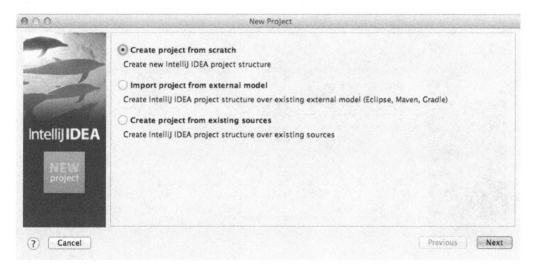

On the next page, we need to fill out some details about our new project. I named my project `MyProcessingSketch`. The type should be set to **Java Module**. IntelliJ IDEA will take care of the location for your project files. It will create the `IdeaProjects` folder for this in your home directory.

The next thing you'll do is to create the source directory for your project. This is where your Java files will be saved. This directory is usually named `src`.

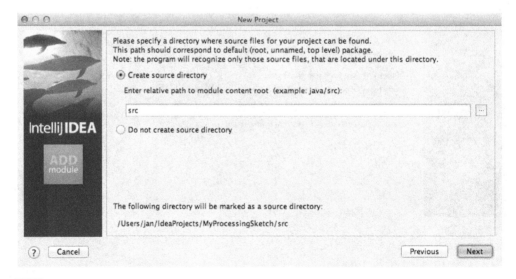

We need to select the right Java Development Kit (JDK) for our project now. Click the **Configure...** button. On the next screen, you need to click the **New** button, and select **JSDK** from the drop-down menu that will appear. On the next window, you just need to click the **Choose** button. IntelliJ IDEA will have selected the directory for the right JSDK for you. The screen should now look like the following screenshot. Click the **Next** button to go to the last screen. You don't need to do anything here but click the **Finish** button.

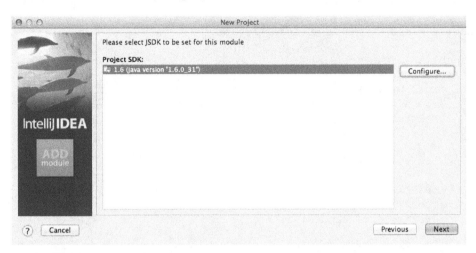

The next thing we need to do is to add the Processing `core.jar` to our project. Go to the **File | Project Structure** menu to show the **Project Structure** window. Pick the **Global Libraries** option from the left-hand side of the screen. Click the yellow **+** icon on the top of the screen and select the `core.jar` file to add it to the project. We discussed how to get this file from the Processing app in the recipes on creating libraries and tools earlier in this chapter. I've placed a copy of the `core.jar` file in a `libs` directory in my `IdeaProjects` folder. Once you've added this file, the window should look like the following screenshot. Click the **OK** button to finish.

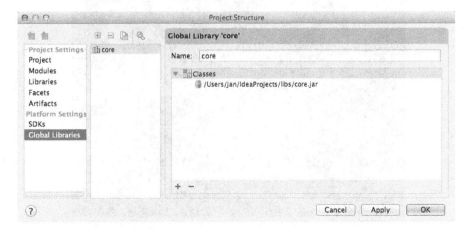

All is done; we can start coding now. Select the **src** directory on the left-hand side in your project, and right-click on it to bring up a menu. Select **New | Java Class** to add a new Java file to the project. We'll start by importing the `processing.core.PApplet` package. Our `MySketch` class should extend the `PApplet` class, so we can use all the functionality from Processing in our sketch.

```
import processing.core.*;

public class MySketch extends PApplet {

  public void setup()
  {
    size( 640, 480 );
    smooth();
    background( 0 );
  }

  public void draw()
  {
    noFill();
    stroke( 255, random( 128, 255 ), 0, 64 );
    strokeWeight( random( 1, 4 ) );

    ellipse( random( width ), random( height ), 30, 30 );
  }
}
```

Once you've finished writing the code, you can run the sketch going to the **Run | Run 'MySketch'** menu. The result should look like the following screenshot:

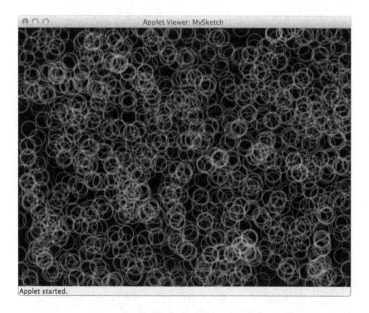

How it works...

The process of creating sketches with IntelliJ IDEA is similar to how we used Processing with Eclipse, before the Processing plug in for Eclipse was made. The only thing you need to do is set up your project, and make sure the Processing `core.jar` file is linked to it. Let's take a look at some of the code we wrote and see how it works.

The first thing we did was import the Processing core, so we access all Processing functions in our sketch.

```
import processing.core.*;
```

We made sure that our `MySketch` class extends the `PApplet` class. This will enable us to run our app as a Processing applet.

```
public class MySketch extends PApplet {}
```

You may have noticed that we used the `public` keyword at the beginning of the `setup()` and `draw()` methods in our class. If we don't make these methods public, our sketch won't run. All other Processing functions can be used just like you would use them in the PDE.

```
public void setup() {}
public void draw() {}
```

These are the main differences to writing a sketch within the PDE. Actually, when you run a sketch from Processing, your `sketch.pde` file will be converted to a Java class. Processing will add the public keywords to your `setup()` and `draw()` functions, and wrap your sketch in a class that extends `PApplet`. When writing sketches in IntelliJ IDEA, you have to do this manually.

Index

Symbols

2D and 3D objects
  mixing 76-78
3D camera
  using 83, 84
  working 85
3D files
  exporting 116-119
3D primitives
  drawing 66, 68
  working 68
3D scene
  lights, using 69-72
3D shapes
  polygon soup, making 73-75
3D sketches
  creating, for web 202-204
  creating, on Android 243, 245
3D space
  about 63-65
  enabling 66
<canvas> tag 207
@@description@@ variable 196
@@height@@ variable 196
@@id@@ variable 196
@@scripts@@ variable 196
@@sketch@@ variable 196
@@source@@ variable 196
.vlw file format 42
@@width@@ variable 196

A

abs() function 21, 144
accelerationEvent() function 236, 238

accelerometer
  about 221
  using 235-238
  working 238
AccelerometerManager class 238
add() method 106
ambientLight() function 72
Android
  3D sketches, creating 243, 245
Android App
  icon, adding 245-247
Android device
  sketch, running 228, 230
  working 230
Android Emulator
  about 221
  sketch, running 224, 225
  working 226, 227
Android mode
  about 15, 221
  accelerometer, using 235-238
  GPS, using 239-242
  screen size and density, accessing 230, 232
  touch interaction, responding 232-234
Android Network Location Provider 243
Android SDK
  downloading 222
  installing 222, 223
  using 224
  working 224
Android UI Guidelines
  URL 247
append() function 99, 101
applications
  exporting 111, 112
arrayCopy() function 99, 102

Thank you for buying
Processing 2: Creative Programming Cookbook

About Packt Publishing

Packt, pronounced 'packed', published its first book "*Mastering phpMyAdmin for Effective MySQL Management*" in April 2004 and subsequently continued to specialize in publishing highly focused books on specific technologies and solutions.

Our books and publications share the experiences of your fellow IT professionals in adapting and customizing today's systems, applications, and frameworks. Our solution based books give you the knowledge and power to customize the software and technologies you're using to get the job done. Packt books are more specific and less general than the IT books you have seen in the past. Our unique business model allows us to bring you more focused information, giving you more of what you need to know, and less of what you don't.

Packt is a modern, yet unique publishing company, which focuses on producing quality, cutting-edge books for communities of developers, administrators, and newbies alike. For more information, please visit our website: www.packtpub.com.

About Packt Open Source

In 2010, Packt launched two new brands, Packt Open Source and Packt Enterprise, in order to continue its focus on specialization. This book is part of the Packt Open Source brand, home to books published on software built around Open Source licences, and offering information to anybody from advanced developers to budding web designers. The Open Source brand also runs Packt's Open Source Royalty Scheme, by which Packt gives a royalty to each Open Source project about whose software a book is sold.

Writing for Packt

We welcome all inquiries from people who are interested in authoring. Book proposals should be sent to author@packtpub.com. If your book idea is still at an early stage and you would like to discuss it first before writing a formal book proposal, contact us; one of our commissioning editors will get in touch with you.

We're not just looking for published authors; if you have strong technical skills but no writing experience, our experienced editors can help you develop a writing career, or simply get some additional reward for your expertise.

OpenCV 2 Computer Vision Application Programming Cookbook

ISBN: 978-1-849513-24-1   Paperback: 304 pages

Over 50 recipes to master this library of programming functions for real-time computer vision

1. Teaches you how to program computer vision applications in C++ using the different features of the OpenCV library

2. Demonstrates the important structures and functions of OpenCV in detail with complete working examples

3. Describes fundamental concepts in computer vision and image processing

WebGL Beginner's Guide

ISBN: 978-1-849691-72-7   Paperback: 376 pages

Become a master of 3D web programming in WebGL and JavaScript

1. Dive headfirst into 3D web application development using WebGL and JavaScript

2. Each chapter is loaded with code examples and exercises that allow the reader to quickly learn the various concepts associated with 3D web development

3. The only software that the reader needs to run the examples is an HTML5 enabled modern web browser. No additional tools needed

Please check **www.PacktPub.com** for information on our titles

Android Database Programming

ISBN: 978-1-849518-12-3   Paperback: 212 pages

Exploit the power of data-centric and data-driven Android applications with this practical tutorial

1. Master the skills to build data-centric Android applications

2. Go beyond just code by challenging yourself to think about practical use-cases with SQLite and others

3. Focus on flushing out high level design concepts, before drilling down into different code examples

Adobe Flash 11 Stage3D (Molehill) Game Programming Beginner's Guide

ISBN: 978-1-849691-68-0   Paperback: 412 pages

A step-by-step guide for creating stunning 3D games in Flash 11 Stage3D (Molehill) using AS3 and AGAL

1. The first book on Adobe's Flash 11 Stage3D, previously codenamed Molehill

2. Build hardware-accelerated 3D games with a blazingly fast frame rate

3. Full of screenshots and ActionScript 3 source code, each chapter builds upon a real-world example game project step-by-step

4. Light-hearted and informal, this book is your trusty sidekick on an epic quest to create your very own 3D Flash game

Please check **www.PacktPub.com** for information on our titles

CPSIA information can be obtained
at www.ICGtesting.com
Printed in the USA
LVHW050044300721
693950LV00009B/474

9 781849 517942